MARCO ⊕ POLO

Tips

IRELAND

Glasgow

North Sea

IRELAND
Dublin

GREAT BRITAIN

Amsterdam

NETHER-LANDS

ATLANTIC

London

BELGIUM

OCEAN

English Channel

FRANCE

The best Insider Tips → p. 4

INSIDER TIP

Best of ... → p. 6

In and around Dublin → p. 32

The South → p. 46

SYMBOLS

INSIDER TIP	Insider Tip
★	Highlight
●●●●	Best of ...
☼	Scenic view
☺	Responsible travel: for ecological or fair trade aspects
(*)	Telephone numbers that are not toll-free

PRICE CATEGORIES HOTELS

Expensive	over 160 euros
Moderate	80–160 euros
Budget	under 80 euros

Prices are valid per night for a double room with breakfast

PRICE CATEGORIES RESTAURANTS

Expensive	over 40 euros
Moderate	20–40 euros
Budget	under 20 euros

Prices are valid for a meal with starter, main course and dessert without drinks

On the cover: Cliffs of Moher: spectacularly dramatic coastline p. 75 | Pub crawl through Dublin p. 41

CONTENTS

The West coast → p. 70

The Northwest → S. 80

The Midlands → p. 88

Road atlas → p. 122

INSIDE BACK COVER:
PULL-OUT MAP →

DID YOU KNOW?
Timeline → p. 12
Local specialities → p. 26
Dog racing → p. 57
Books & films → p. 94
Currency converter → p. 115
Budgeting → p. 117
Weather in Dublin → p. 119

MAPS IN THE GUIDEBOOK
(124 A1) Page numbers and coordinates refer to the road atlas. Coordinates are also given for places, that are not marked in the road atlas
(0) Site/address located off the map
(U A1) Coordinates for the map of Dublin in the back cover. Maps for Limerick and Cork in the back cover

PULL-OUT MAP
(A–B 2–3) Refers to the removable pull-out map
(a–b 2–3) Refers to the additional map on the pull-out map

The best MARCO POLO Insider Tips

Our top 15 Insider Tips

INSIDER TIP Smelling salts...

To see the spectacular natural wonder of the Cliffs of Moher (up to 656 ft high) from the boat is a particularly intense experience. An added bonus of this trip, buffeted by the waves of the Atlantic: you can observe puffins and other sea birds nesting at other inaccessible sites (photo above) → p. 75

INSIDER TIP Teatime in the park

Lunch or afternoon tea at Muckross Garden Restaurant in Killarney: the large terrace with views of the old greenhouses and the Victorian landscaped park of the manor house is unique → p. 60

INSIDER TIP Peninsula in the rough Atlantic

At some 60 miles, the Ring of Beara is a great alternative to the better-known (and oh, so busy) Ring of Kerry; also, the Beara Peninsula boasts lush vegetation and a dramatic coastline → p. 62

INSIDER TIP A pub in the far west

Small, unpretentious and famous with all fans of Irish folk: the owner of the spick-and-span Matt Molloy's pub in Westport is Matt Molloy, no less, who's been playing the flute with the Irish band The Chieftains for the past 30 years → p. 78

INSIDER TIP In the summer time

Fans of the great poet W B Yeats meet every summer in Sligo for the two-week Yeats International Summer School → p. 81

INSIDER TIP B & B in the castle

The classiest B&B in all of Ireland, without a doubt: reside between antiques in the wings of historic Bantry House – some rooms even have a view of Bantry Bay (photo right) → p. 55

INSIDER TIP Look to the stars

Once used to determine the temperature of the moon, this ancient telescope is still working perfectly – get a closer look at Birr Castle → **p. 92**

INSIDER TIP **Shopping in the manor house**

Jams in Victorian terracotta pots, sugar rock in luminous colours: the products for sale at the Avoca Store in Powerscourt House are a visual treat → **p. 45**

INSIDER TIP **By cable car onto the lonely island**

Nothing for scaredy-cats: the dramatic 30-metre cable-car trip leads across the spectacular Dursey Sound to the rocky Atlantic islet of Dursey Island → **p. 62**

INSIDER TIP **For lovers of Irish folk music**

Find out how a bodhrán drum is hand-made the traditional way from goat skin in Malachy Kearns' workshop in the harbour town of Roundstone → **p. 76**

INSIDER TIP **Pure nature**

Mountains, brooks and waterfalls, mist, moss and sheep: the picturesque valley of The Vee is nearly too pretty to be true → **p. 101**

INSIDER TIP **Amongst dolphins and seals**

Captain Raymond Ross knows where to best observe marine mammals. Joining a boat tour in Kenmare Bay guarantees a close encounter with nature and typically Irish humour → **p. 108**

INSIDER TIP **Whiskey tasting**

The Old Jameson Distillery counts amongst the oldest and most important in Ireland. Visit the former distillery in Dublin and taste some excellent whiskey → **p. 36**

INSIDER TIP **Jazz & folk**

The best of pub culture: traditional Irish music to sing along to several times a week at the Sheela-na-Gig in Sligo → **p. 84**

INSIDER TIP **Irish cottage Life**

Find out how people lived in rural Ireland 100 to 300 years ago at the Folk Village Museum in Glencolumbkille → **p. 87**

BEST OF ...

FOR FREE

● **Ormond Castle**
Nearly all of Ireland's castles charge an entrance fee. The pretty Renaissance-era *Ormond Castle* in the small town of Carrick-on-Suir is a pleasing exception → **p. 93**

● **Old Masters**
An oasis of calm and the arts, Dublin's National Gallery is the place to enjoy European masterpieces and to have arts students guide you through the exhibition rooms – for free → **p. 36**

● **People-watching on trendy markets**
Hobnob with hipsters without paying: in Dublin's trendy Temple Bar quarter, not one but three markets on Saturday and Sunday give you the chance to meet the hip folk: the fashion crowd at *Cow's Lane Fashion Market*, the sustainable foodies at *Temple Bar Food Market* and the intellectuals at *Temple Bar Book Market* → **p. 43**

● **Art at the customs house**
The small charming *Crawford Art Gallery* in Cork is off the beaten tourist track. Enjoy the calm and stylish atmosphere, and take in paintings and precious artefacts found during excavations in the region – no charge! → **p. 49**

● **Street parades for St Patrick**
On 17 March, as well as the days before and after, the *St Patrick's Festival* becomes the hub of Dublin public life. Experience how the Irish celebrate their patron saint: with street parades, dance and colourful events (photo) → **p. 110**

● **Art in neoclassical surroundings**
Free of charge: at the *Royal Hospital* in Dublin, Ireland's largest neoclassical building, fabulously beautiful rooms are given over to the *Irish Museum of Modern Art (IMMA)* with its high-calibre modern artworks, as well as an arts centre → **p. 37**

●●●● Dots in guidebook refer to 'Best of ...' tips

ONLY IN IRELAND
Unique experiences

● *Ireland's rough beauty*

To experience the wild side of Ireland, head for the Aran Islands off the west coast. Discover *Dun Aengus*, an Iron Age fort perched on the edge of a cliff above the Atlantic, buffeted by the wind for over 2500 years now → p. 74

● *Pubs: places of inspiration*

Ireland's greatest writers had a stool with their name on it, and Irish musicians played their first gig in pubs. The *Dublin Literary Pub Crawl* and the *Musical Pub Crawl* through the nightlife hub of Temple Bar (photo) allows you to follow in their footsteps → p. 41

● *Celtic high crosses*

Come real close to Celtic spirituality: the high crosses standing in the grounds of the ruined monastery of *Monasterboice* are the highest – at over six metres – and arguably the most beautiful in all of Ireland → p. 45

● *Gone to the dogs*

At the dog races, in Cork for instance, you sit next to betting harbour labourers and fishermen, students and housewives. Cheer on the greyhounds with them, and indulge in the passion of the common man, which today runs through all social levels → p. 57

● *Folk music with country folk*

Every year in August, folk music lovers meet at the *Fleadh Cheoil na hEireann*. Do as the Irish fans do: make music and have a dance at the many small festivals in villages and small towns → p. 111

● *Garden delights*

For two weeks in June, garden owners who have come together under the *West Cork Garden Trail* umbrella open their gates, giving insights into the fantastical world of wild flowers, orchids, rhododendrons, tropical trees and Himalayan cedars → p. 58

● *Round tower in the ruined monastery*

Mystical Ireland: to admire the most beautiful of the country's nearly millennial freestanding round towers, head for Glendalough. The tower belongs to the crumbling monastic settlement of the same name, one of the most mysterious places in the country → p. 44

ONLY IN

BEST OF ...

● *Light at the end of the tunnel*
You won't get wet diving into the mystery of the megalithic tomb of *Newgrange*. Once arrived at the heart of the passage tomb, some 5000 years old, an artificial ray of light demonstrates what happens naturally at winter solstice (photo) → p. 45

● *Stay with the Count*
Breathe in Irish history in the beautiful, charmingly dusty family seat of the Earls of Bantry. Stroll through *Bantry House* and check out the family treasures at your own pace → p. 55

● *Dead Poets Society*
In the *Dublin Writers Museum* you are right inside the universe of literary Dublin: even the waistcoat of James Joyce is exhibited here. And the in-house bookstore is a treasure trove for out-of-print books by Irish authors → p. 35

● *Dining medieval-style*
At a banquet at historic *Bunratty Castle* you are a guest of the Middle Ages. Damsels entertain with ethereal song, the table is laden with hearty meat dishes and mead → p. 69

● *What a fine maze!*
Shopping in the historic town palace and the roofed-over atrium: meet Dublin's moneyed crowd in the exclusive shops, trendy cafés and restaurants of the *Powerscourt Centre* → p. 40

● *Going underground*
A worthwhile descent: over the course of two million years, nature has shaped *Aillwee Cave* into a massive cave maze with countless stalagmites, stalactites and a subterranean waterfall → p. 74

RAIN

RELAX AND CHILL OUT
Take it easy and spoil yourself

● *Trotting through the park*

Take a jaunt through *Killarney National Park* in a horse-drawn carriage to romantic places on the lake. On cooler days, plaid woolly blankets will keep you warm; the drivers will keep you entertained any day (photo) → p. 58

● *Seaweed in Sligo*

Irish algae have been rediscovered as a source of true rejuvenation: bathe in them or have a massage with hot herbal bags or hot stones at the *Voya Seaweed Baths*. Here, the traditional healing powers of the sea are combined with a good dose of design and zeitgeist → p. 84

● *Teatime in the terrace café*

The terrace café in the pretty landscaped park of *Powerscourt Gardens* affords views of fountains and sculptures that are best enjoyed with an Irish coffee and an apple pie fresh out of the oven, with a dollop of clotted cream → p. 45

● *Enlightenment included*

Occupying a prominent position above the steep coastline of the Beara Peninsula, the Tibetan Buddhist *Dzogchen Beara* Centre welcomes anybody for daily meditation classes or retreats lasting a weekend or longer → p. 62

● *Cocktail in Killarney*

You won't find a more beautiful place for a sundowner in all Killarney: on the terrace of *The Europe* design hotel, lake and mountains seem within your grasp → p. 62

● *Yoga by the sea*

Nobody is too old or too unfit to stretch their limbs at the *Burren Yoga Centre* near Kinvara. The place has not only a friendly atmosphere but also – according to New Age followers – a strong force field → p. 75

● *Spa with a green view*

From the *Kenmare Park Hotel* spa see Japanese-style zen gardens featuring bamboo and pebbles, and relax on top-designer lounge furniture → p. 64

INTRODUCTION

DISCOVER IRELAND!

In Ireland, many a small chat begins with a standard subject: the weather. The remark *'Isn't it a nice day today?'* is not only the perfect excuse for a conversation for the locals, who are always up for a chat, but also shows their resilience in weather matters. If even a gloomy, cloudy morning is hailed as a great day, you won't be surprised to see school kids on the Emerald Isle meeting the occasionally grim cold of the winter months with nothing more than knee socks and skirts. The changeable weather, runs the pragmatic wisdom, has a lot of good to it, and after all, it doesn't rain in the pub, does it now?

An impressive vocabulary is available to differentiate between the size of the raindrops and the associated blowing wind. The weather forecast has dozens of names for rain. 'Fine scattered drizzle', which even has its own expression in the Irish language, bears much of the responsibility for the fact that Ireland is so beautifully green. Lying in the sea off the northwest coast of Europe like a moss-covered rock, the island with its wind-buffeted coasts, barren high plateaus and lush vegetation forms a unique

Photo: Rocky cove in Baltimore

Remnant of the Christian past: the ruined monastic complex of Glendalough

natural landscape. Anyone driving or cycling across the island along occasionally rutted and narrow roads will notice that the *forty shades of green* immortalised in song are anything but a cliché. The fast change of rain and sun also ensures a steady supply of rainbows.

Changeable is also the right word for the economic situation of the past few years. While Ireland was considered the poorhouse of Europe up to joining the EU in 1973, from the mid-1990s onwards the country experienced an economic boom, earning it the epithet of Celtic Tiger and making it one of the wealthiest countries in the EU. Since 2008 things have been going downhill again, and fast. In early 2011, Ireland

400 BC–2nd century AD
Celts come to Ireland from the Continent, displacing the people already in place and forming small kingdoms. Trade with Britannia and Roman Gaul leads to Christianisation

8th century
Christianity spreads across the whole country, schooling is introduced, religious leaders obtain equal standing to secular rulers

1534
Henry VIII, King of England, subdues Ireland in the Battle of Maynooth

1845–48
Potato blight and harvest failures lead to famine. A million people die, another million emigrate

needed a EU cash injection of billions. The global economic crisis particularly affected Ireland, bringing with it the collapse of the local construction industry as well as a drastic decline in exports. Unemployment and emigration are on the rise, and ever more sectors of the population are threatened by poverty. The public mood reached an absolute nadir when various investigative commissions revealed that for decades, Roman-Catholic priests, sheltered by bishops, had mistreated and sexually abused children and adolescents. Tens of thousands of cases have become known – a shock for the still overwhelmingly Catholic population.

Another source of conflict lies in Northern Ireland, the Troubles, which have their historic roots in the 17th-century 'Plantations' of mainly Scottish Protestants in Ulster loyal to Britain, and which still threaten to erupt. The bloody unrest and civil war following the partition of the island (1921), and the later IRA (Irish Republican Army) bombing campaign spread to London and the British mainland. It took the 1998 Good Friday Agreement, aiming to give autonomy to Northern Ireland and freeing prisoners in exchange for IRA disarmament, to get a peaceful solution underway. In 2005, the IRA leadership decided to end the armed struggle. This doesn't cover splinter groups like the Real IRA however, responsible for the 1998 Omagh atrocity where 30 people died. Peace in Northern Ireland remains a delicate flower.

The Celtic Tiger takes a nosedive

1916
The Easter Rising is struck down. The Sinn Féin ('We Ourselves') party proclaims an Irish parliament. England replies with armed force; formation of the IRA

1921
Ireland is partitioned

1969
Violence between Protestants and Catholics in Northern Ireland, more British troops are sent, the IRA supports the Catholic defence

1973
Ireland joins the EC (European Community), benefiting immensely over the course of the next generation

A therapy to combat depressing news stories since time immemorial is to chat in the pub. As in the UK, here the heavily tattooed construction worker props up the counter next to a bank employee in his ironed designer shirt. The Irish also enjoy socialising over sports, and particularly enjoy golf. Most golf courses boast lush green vegetation, and not a few also a dream location with views of the raging sea and dramatic cliffs.

Young and old meet at the racetrack

A passion transcending generations and social class is betting. A high number of Dubliners name greyhound races as their favourite pastime. The evening events of the dog racetrack of Shelbourne Park attract a throng of young and old, men in corduroy suits and flat cap, youngsters in baggy tracksuit bottoms and dolled-up women accompanied by their female friends. Only a few decades ago, horse races and betting were considered the domain of the wealthier section of society, while dog races were associated with the working class. There is another tradition that has survived: the favourite pastime of many rural women remains bingo.

What makes Ireland so endearing, alongside the open and outgoing people, is the country's natural beauty. The island boasts countless prehistoric and medieval cultural treasures: mystic places imbued with power where stones associated with druidic practices reach for the sky, alongside ancient tomb chambers and ruined nameless castles from Norman times. Amongst the extraordinary prehistoric survivals is *Dun Aengus*, a stone fort on the Aran Islands, as well as a burial chamber in Newgrange in Co. Meath that is around 5000 years old. Every year on 21 December a magical lightshow is revealed when the rays of the sun enter the passage through a cunningly constructed opening. Early Christianisation left its traces in high crosses, round towers and monastic complexes. Thus an important monastic settlement formed around the year 1000 in Glendalough (Co. Wicklow), while the *Gallarus Oratory* on the Dingle Peninsula dates to the 8th century.

At the most beautiful spots of the country, British nobility once built their mansion houses, beautiful country estates which over the course of time appeared to fuse with the landscape around. Typical are the entrance portals surrounded by climbing ivy and vines, their tall lattice windows, quarrystone mews and turreted gatehouses, as

2002
Introduction of the euro

2005
Changeover to the metric system

2007
After 38 years, the British army ends its deployment in Northern Ireland

2010
Ireland narrowly escapes state bankruptcy

2011
New elections in the wake of the debt crisis: Enda Kenny of the Fine Gael party becomes prime minister; Ireland receives billions in financial aid from the EU.

Irish living rooms: pubs such as The Small Bridge on the Dingle Peninsula

well as their Victorian-style conservatories. Many of the Big Houses, castles, manor houses and fortified houses today open their gates to a paying public, or serve as restaurants or hotels. The interior is usually original: fireplaces as tall as a man, wood-panelled libraries, gently curving staircases, as well as rooms furnished with antiques.

A trip to Ireland is also an encounter with a different concept of time. 'When God made time, he made enough of it', would sum up the ap-

In the spring, pastures take on a luminous deep green

proach of a lot of Irish people. All it means is: take it easy. For instance when the boat service to one of the small islands can only run again the following day, or when those drops start to fall and the planned excursion is literally rained off. Ireland is particularly beautiful in the spring, when huge rhododendrons, extensive fuchsia groves and deep-green pastures gleam in the sun. Bird colonies nest along the steep coastline, the magic of the light defying description. The western coast attracts most visitors. One of the main attractions in the south is the Ring of Kerry, a breathtaking road following the sea, without a doubt one of Ireland's most beautiful routes. The cliffs and mountains of granite and quartz lend the western coast (Co. Clare and Galway) a rough edge. The east has dune-fringed beaches and high plateaus covered in heather, while the northwest is *Gaeltacht* country – meaning those regions where Irish is still spoken on a regular basis. Wherever you meet the barren beauty of the upland bogs and unspoilt mountainsides, you will hear *Failte go Eireann* – Welcome to Ireland.

WHAT'S HOT

1 Wellness from the sea

Active health bomb Seaweed is the island's natural wellness weapon. The plant's iodine content can be 20,000 times higher than in seawater, lending it a particularly high therapeutic force. During a *Voya Herbal Bag Massage*, the *Monart* health farm wraps its spa guests in a blend of herbs and seaweed *(The Still, Enniscorthy, Co. Wexford, www.monart.ie, photo)*. All the rage at the *Temple Spa* is the *Phyto-Marine Body Treatment* with shredded seaweed *(Horseleap, Moate, Co. Westmeath, www. templespa.ie)*.

Gaelic football

2

Irish national sport Gaelic Football spans tradition and trend with ease. Tens of thousands of fans follow the ball being kicked and thrown at the *Croke Park Stadium (Cusack Stand, Dublin, photo)*. The sport combines the velocity of football with the toughness of rugby. The fun is organised by the *Gaelic Athletic Association (www.gaa.ie)*. To find out all you need to know about the sport head for the museum at Croke Park *(St Joseph's Avenue, Dublin, www.museum.gaa.ie)*.

Movie mania

3

Eldorado for cinema lovers Statistically, more people go to the cinema in Dublin than in any other city in Europe. The latest trend: independent fillums made in Ireland. *Filmbase* supports film makers with material, studios and workshops *(Curved Street, Dublin, photo)*, and the *Irish Film Institute (6 Eustace Street, Dublin, www.ifi.ie)* also contributes to the current trend with small and bigger film productions and two screens. A new thing is Ireland's first mobile cinema, crisscrossing the island in a truck *(www.cinemobile.net)*.

Donkey trek

On the back of a donkey Find Irish happiness on the back of one of Ireland's tough and sweet donkeys. In the olden days they were used for transporting peat. Today, the fuel is swapped for luggage, allowing visitors to explore the island's hidden beauties on the back of the cuddly, if occasionally stubborn animals. Accommodation is available at cosy guesthouses. The expanses of forest and heather around the *An Sibin Riding Centre* are ideal for donkey trekking *(Mountshannon, Derryoran East Whitegate, Co. Clare, www.irish horseriding.com)*. The *Slieve Aughty Riding Centre* offers treks from one overnight stop to the next *(Kylebrack West, Loughrea, Co. Galway, www.riding-centre.com, photo)*.

Gourmet boom

New cookery classes The Irish got to know haute cuisine abroad. Now, the creation of fine dishes is booming on the Emerald Isle, with gourmet trips and cookery workshops ever more popular. The most famous place to learn is *Ballymaloe Cookery School* with its own organic farm *(Shanagarry, Co. Cork, www. cookingisfun.ie)*. The smallest cookery school is situated on idyllic Heir Island. Over two days, two participants learn the secrets of the kitchen at the *Island Cottage Cookery School (Skibbereen, Co. Cork, www.islandcottage.com, photo)*. The *Pangur Bán Cookery School* in Letterfrack boasts a spectacular location between the Atlantic and the Twelve Bens mountains *(Connemara, Co. Galway, www.pangurban.com)*.

IN A NUTSHELL

BOGS

A whiff of peat smoke hangs over Irish villages, rising up from bogs and fireplaces. At the beginning of the 19th century, 15 per cent of the island's surface was still covered in peat bogs. Alongside industrial extraction through *Bord na Mona*, founded in 1946, a state-run board managing peat-fuelled power stations, turf is still cut the traditional way by hand. Many areas are now protected, such as Clara Bog in Co. Offaly, which is 7 metres deep and 10,000 years old.

CATHOLIC CHURCH

Ireland is still a bastion of Catholicism. 88 per cent of the population are Catholic, and the church has been involved in education and the social sector for centuries. This was why the shock resonated so deeply when the extent of the abuse scandal became known in 2010. From the 1930s into the 1990s, up to 14,500 children and young people fell victim to sexual abuse by Catholic clergy. Four bishops have had to resign after covering up the abuses.

While the official church has lost credibility, large numbers of Irish believers make the pilgrimage to Knock, the Irish version of Lourdes in France. Every year, the Co. Mayo village in the West of Ireland attracts about 1.5 million pilgrims. Knock became one of the world's most important sites of pilgrimage, after the Virgin Mary allegedly appeared to fifteen faithful in 1879, bathing the area with luminous light. Today, Knock not only boasts

Photo: Peat sods on a Connemara bog

A lot of weather: from high-lying peat bogs to subtropical climes – the Irish know and love this kind of contrast

a large basilica, but also an international airport (Knock Airport).

ECONOMY

In 1973, when it entered the European Union, Ireland was the community's poorest member. In 2005, following 35 billion of euros in subsidies and strong economic development, the country was one of the richest states – not just in the EU but world-wide. However, the 'Celtic Tiger' was brought to its knees by the global financial crisis. The property boom triggered by very low interest rates burst its bubble, and the banking crisis rapidly led to a state debt crisis. In 2008, when the country was hit by the recession, unemployment rose to over 13 per cent. Since then, the economic crisis has had the Emerald Isle in its grip. Beginning in 2010, the rating agencies kept relentlessly downgrading Ireland, and in 2011 a threatened state bankruptcy was only averted by an EU injection of billions of euros. Nobody assumes that the economy will recover in the foreseeable future – despite rigorous austerity measures touching the welfare sector too, as well as tax increases.

FAMINE

The Great Famine, the biggest catastrophe in Irish history, took place between 1845 and 1849. The roots of the problem lay in terrible poverty, provoked by the exploitation of Irish estates by English landlords. The Irish were left with the potato as the main part of their diet. There had been famines before, over a dozen potato blights of varying extent between 1816 und 1842. In the autumn of 1845, the potatoes were once again affected by a fungus. In this and the following years the harvests that formed the livelihood of the people were completely devastated. One million of the 8.5 million Irish died, and the same number again were forced to emigrate.

GAELIC

Gaeltacht areas are those regions in the West where Irish Gaelic is still spoken today and where traditional mores and customs have been preserved. A branch of the Celtic language family presumably reached Ireland in the 1st century BC. In the 19th century, the British replaced Irish with English. Today, Ireland is officially bilingual. About five to ten per cent of the Irish are able to speak at least some of the language of their ancestors. Whilst only about two per cent of the population speak Irish on a daily basis, Gaelic is experiencing a revival at the moment. Amongst cultured city folk too it has become fashionable to support Gaelic culture. Particularly active here is the Seachtain na Gaeilge association, which stages Irish-language readings and musical evenings in Irish, as well as a ten-day festival in March *(www.snag.ie)* where everything revolves around Gaelic heritage.

GARDENS

The mild Irish climate, favoured by the warm Gulf Stream and frequent short rain showers, ensures a unique vegetation. While Ireland may resemble one big landscaped garden, many Irish have turned their private gardens into horticultural gems, which they present to the public. Alongside generously laid-out cottage gardens, enchanted monastery gardens and Zen oases, discover famous sculpture parks and so-called *fermes ornées* combining agriculture and horticulture. The latter shelter livestock threatened with extinction and grow heirloom vegetables, such as Larchill Arcadian Garden in County Kildare *(www. larchhill.ie)*. For an in-depth description of publicly accessible gardens, see *www. castlesgardensireland.com.*

A trend imported from Britain is the enthusiasm for organised garden tours lasting several days (e.g. through *www. essenceofireland.ie*). RTE One, the island's oldest TV channel, produces one garden programme after the other. For a beautiful coffee-table book look no further than The Gardens of Ireland, where British garden photographer Melanie Eclare presents 20 extraordinary gardens and their owners.

HORSES

Ireland is a paradise for horse lovers, and not only because the island boasts the most beautiful riding trails and places, e.g. stretches of beach, for cantering. Three very popular breeds are native to the island: Irish Hunters are a cross between thoroughbred and the Irish Draught horse; the robust Irish Tinker (originally a work and draught horse used by the Irish itinerant population) are considered excellent hunting and eventing horses; and Connemara ponies are particularly agile. Every year in October, horse lovers from all over the world make the pilgrimage to the Midlands, to Ballinasloe, for Europe's oldest and biggest horse fair – with funfair and tournaments (www.ballisnasloeoctober fair.com).

LITERATURE

The Irish don't just enjoy telling stories, they are also masters at putting them down on paper. The land of poets and writers, Ireland can boast four Nobel Prize winners for literature: William Butler Yeats received it in 1923, Bernard Shaw 1925, Samuel Beckett in 1969 and Seamus Heaney in 1995. Other Irish writers are no less famous: Jonathan Swift, Sean O'Casey, Oscar Wilde, Brendan Behan, Flann O'Brien and James Joyce. The last-named became famous with his Dublin novel Ulysses, published in 1918, to this day considered groundbreaking for modern literature. Currently Anne Enright, John Banville and Colum McCann garner the highest literary accolades. Irish novels and plays deal with idealism and humanity, ranging stylistically between emphatic poetry and often-subtle satire.

MUSIC

Not only are the Irish great story-tellers, but also accomplished musicians. Traditional instruments are the accordion (or 'box'), the tin whistle, the fiddle, the bodhrán hand drum, violin, flute und *uilleann* pipes, the Irish version of the bagpipe. Musicians meet for sessions, in Ireland also called *seisiun*, often featuring boisterous singing, dancing and playing. Founded in 1962, The Dubliners enjoy legendary status; in the same year, five musicians formed the folk band The Chieftains, successful to this day. Since 1976, Dublin rock band U2 with lead singer Bono has held sway in

Irish pop music. Belfast-born jazz, blues and country singer Van Morrison enjoys worldwide recognition. Bob Geldorf with his Boomtown Rats, the folk-punk band The Pogues, singers Sinéad O'Connor and Enya have all left their mark on the island's music scene, not to forget the boy bands Boyzone and Westlife.

A typical instrument in Irish music is the fiddle

NATIONAL PARKS

The six national parks, managed by the National Parks and Wildlife Service (NPWS), shelter many rare animals, amongst them golden eagles released into the wild, as well as Ireland's largest herd of red deer. Alongside Killarney National Park, Connemara National Park, Ballycroy National Park, Burren National Park and Wicklow Mountains National Park, Glenveagh National Park *(www.glenveaghnationalpark.ie)* with its bogs, lakes and forests spanning over 60 square miles is the country's largest and most fascinating. Lying in the Derryveagh Mountains in County Donegal, the wonderful and eminently hikeable landscape of lakes and hills was made over to the Irish State in 1983 by its owner at the time, the American Henry McIlhenny. The visitor centre of the freely accessible park lies at the northern end of Lough Veagh.

POPULATION

With the Great Famine of 1845–48 at the latest, Europe's poorhouse became a classic country of emigrants. Between the 1990s and about 2007, many Irish returned to their home country to take advantage of the booming economy. Ireland is a young nation; the average age of the 4.4 million inhabitants hovers around 35. Ten per cent of the population are now migrants, half of them of African or Asian heritage. The Republic of Ireland counts amongst the least densely populated countries in Europe, with each square mile only inhabited by 150 people. A third of the population lives in Greater Dublin, so that large areas appear near-devoid of

Horseracing combines two Irish passions: horses and betting

people. 60 per cent of all Irish live in cities.

ST PATRICK

Ireland's patron saint represents the most important figurehead of Irish Catholicism – which is why the most common name in Ireland is Patrick (Paddy). Born around 385, probably in Wales, Patrick was taken by force to the Emerald Isle by pirates around the year 400. Fleeing to France, Patrick joined the priesthood and returned to Ireland in 432 as a missionary. Using the tripartite shamrock, Patrick explained the Holy Trinity to the Irish. The Croagh Patrick mountain, on whose summit the saint is said to have fasted for 40 days in 441,

banishing all snakes to the sea, became a place of pilgrimage. On 17 March 461 Patrick died in Northern Ireland. To this day, that date is commemorated as the Irish national holiday St Patrick's Day – with exuberant parties and parades.

TROUBLES

The roots of the conflict in Northern Ireland go back to the 12th century, when Anglo-Normans began the conquest of Ireland. After the First World War and centuries of denial of rights and oppression, when Protestant settlers displaced the native Catholic Irish, the IRA (Irish Republican Army) fought British occupation. The result was partition. Since 1921, Ireland has been divided in two: the independent Republic of Ireland with Dublin as capital, and Northern Ireland (capital: Belfast), which continues to remain part of the United Kingdom. However, the inner divisions in Northern Ireland remained too: to this day, Catholic nationalists feel oppressed by the Protestant majority, with many aiming to be part of a united Irish Republic, while Protestant unionists want to remain part of the United Kingdom. In 1969 the conflict escalated, when the Northern Irish city of Derry witnessed street battles between Protestants and Catholics. The 1970s in particular saw numerous IRA bomb attacks. All in all, thousands died in sectarian violence. In 2005, the IRA vowed to leave their violent past behind, but attacks by splinter groups and bomb hoaxes still take place. In 1998, the Republic of Ireland dropped its constitutional claim of reunification with the North. At the same time border controls between the North and the South fell. It is debatable however whether the long fight of Irish republicans for independence, which is more than just a religious conflict, is truly over.

FOOD & DRINK

Up until recently, Irish cuisine was not exactly known for its variety. Restaurant menus mainly featured meat dishes served up with fries and vegetables.

In terms of culinary development, though, things have been changing for quite a while already. The Slow Food movement promoting enjoyable, conscious and regional food has arrived in Ireland too. Its most prominent representative is Darina Allen, who is very well known in Ireland. The famous TV chef and author of over a dozen cookery books is one of the pioneers of a 'new' Irish cuisine. At her Ballymaloe Cookery School in Shanagarry she shares her enjoyment of all things food-related and shows how Irish classics may be refined using only the best Irish produce. Even humble porridge can turn into a culinary epiphany at the breakfast table when the oatmeal is prepared with freshly ground grains and fresh cream.

The humble potato, for centuries part of the day-to-day Irish diet, offers an endless range of variations in the ways it can be prepared. There is also a large selection of fish and seafood specialities. Oysters (relatively inexpensive in Ireland), lobster, mussels, crabs, as well as all kinds of fish (amongst them specialities such as shark, tuna and sea bass) appear on the menus. These days there is a great variety of speciality cheeses too. The old art of cheesemaking has been rediscovered. Some of the best *farmhouse cheeses* include *Gubbeen,* a semi-hard cow's-milk cheese, and *Gigginstown,* a

Photo: Pub in Dublin

Much more than just Irish stew and Guinness: try the many kinds of fish and crustaceans from Ireland's lakes and rivers

raw-milk cheese. *Irish goat,* a brie-like goat's cheese, has nothing to fear from its Mediterranean rivals. Other recommended varieties are *Cashel blue* and *Burren gold* as well as *Gabriel* (traditional mountain cheese similar to Gruyère) and *Desmond,* of a softer texture. *Cais nan deise* is a hard cheese with a nutty flavour. Prices for restaurant meals are fairly high, often only starting at 15 euros. One saving grace for those on a budget are tourist menus, consisting of three courses at a fixed price *(15–20 euros).* You can

recognise restaurants offering this kind of menu by a small green sign showing a face with a chef's hat with *special value, tourist menu* written on it. What you get is Irish and international fare of middling quality. The higher-end restaurants will usually place you in the lounge or at the bar first to have a pre-dinner drink, before showing you to the table. Hotel gastronomy knows no days of rest, and in season (June to September) restaurants too will usually be open all days of the week, if often only for dinner.

LOCAL SPECIALITIES

DISHES

▶ **Barmbrack** – rich tea/fruit cake traditionally enjoyed around Christmas
▶ **Boxty** – potato pancake made of a blend of grated raw potato and mash
▶ **Coddle** – traditional stew of potatoes, sausage, onions and bacon
▶ **Colcannon** – mashed potato with cabbage, perhaps refined with cream or also with leeks and onions
▶ **Crubeen** – pig's trotters, well seasoned and smoked, also salted
▶ **Fried woodcock** – game bird wrapped in a slice of bacon
▶ **Irish stew** – national dish of potatoes, white cabbage, lamb and usually carrots
▶ **Seafood** – look out for high-quality seafood of all kinds, from oysters, prawns (e.g. Dublin Bay prawns) and lobster to salmon, monkfish and much more
▶ **Seaweed** – popular varieties are the delicious purple dulse and the greyish carrageen, a thickening agent and also used to brew up with honey for a cold-defying alternative to Lemsip
▶ **Smoked salmon** – light-coloured and expensive wild, farmed usually pink and fatter
▶ **Sodabread** – crumbly round bread made with buttermilk and bicarbonate of soda, delicious with Irish butter

DRINKS

▶ **Cider** – the best brand of the fizzy apple drink with low alcohol is Bulmer's from Co. Tipperary; look out for their pear cider
▶ **Guinness** – the most famous brand of the dark stout beers
▶ **Irish coffee** – strong hot coffee with brown sugar, a slug of whiskey and a whipped-cream top (photo left)
▶ **Spring water** – Ballygowan's is the most famous brand of Irish bottled water

Vegetarians are well catered for these days, even if sometimes the default dish, goat's cheese and red onion tart, can get a bit tiring. For information on special restaurants and events see *www.fabulousfoodtrails.ie.*

The full Irish breakfast is quite substantial: tea or coffee with orange juice, porridge (oatmeal) and cereals, eggs and sausages, as well as bacon. All this comes with *soda bread* or *brown bread* and toast. During lunch hour, the Irish will often only take a light snack, with much of the working population heading for the nearest pub for a soup or sandwich. Eateries in the town centres are usually full at this time. The main meal is taken in the evening.

The Irish drink more tea than any other nation in the world and enjoy their cuppa with fresh milk and sugar. Two well-known tea companies and expert blenders are Barry (Cork) and Bewley (Dublin). Just as in Britain, the pub in Ireland is a lot more than a watering hole. The public house is a meeting place to chat and to make music, to gossip about politics, make your opinions heard and listen to others. People from all social sectors and all age groups meet at the pub, formerly (in the countryside today still) mainly men. Pubs in Ireland are split in two: the lounge, where ladies sit with their husbands or chat with a female friend, and the bar proper where drinks are pulled and served. Again as in Britain, you order your drinks at the bar and pay straight away. Pubs are usually open between 10am and midnight, on Sundays between 4 and 11pm. Technically, young people under 18 are not allowed in, children are not well seen either, and the minimum age for occupying a seat at the bar is 21. Pubs and restaurants are subject to a smoking ban that is well observed.

While Guinness might be known as the Irish beer, all it is is a brand name for dark porter beer (stout); other popular brands are Beamish and Murphy's. If you order a stout, or any beer really, you will be given a pint (about half a litre). If you find this too much, order half a pint or simply a glass. The range of beers is similar to the UK otherwise: bitters, light lagers and ales. Smithwick's ale (called

'Kilkenny' abroad as non-native speakers struggle with the pronunciation!) is a popular choice between a fizzy lager and heavy stout. Last not least, Irish whiskey – spelt with an 'e' – is distilled three times as opposed to twice (as

Social meeting place: pubs in Kenmare

in the case of most Scotch whiskies), which gives it a smoother texture. The Bushmills distillery recently celebrated its 400th anniversary and has a good range of vintage malts. Other famous brands are Jameson's, Tullamore Dew and Paddy's, and there are plans to set up a new boutique distillery on the Dingle Peninsula. Peated whiskey, while not made in Connemara, is available under the Connemara brand name. The famous moonshine potato spirit, poteen, is now available perfectly legally.

SHOPPING

Large department stores are only available in Dublin, Galway, Cork and Limerick. But don't worry, the small shops specialising for instance in jewellery featuring ancient Celtic motifs, film posters or handmade soaps are much more interesting anyway. Often you'll still find stores that stock everything the rural population needs to survive: from tobacco and fishing twine to the daily newspaper.

Also worth a visit are teashops and coffeeshops serving as bookshops, galleries or shop exhibition space.

Normally, shops are open between 9 or 9.30am and 5.30 or 6pm. On Sundays only a few supermarkets are open.

CERAMICS & JEWELLERY

Art shops and art galleries offer a large selection of pictures and ceramics, crystalware, printed fabrics and jewellery. The centuries-old Claddagh design (two hands holding a crowned heart) is used on rings and earrings. You'll also find replicas of old Celtic fibulas.

CULINARY SOUVENIRS

A souvenir suitable to take in hand-luggage is wild smoked salmon, a rare delicacy. It also contains less fat than farmed salmon, which often owes its red colour to chemical food additives. Another option is to stock up on farmhouse cheeses made with raw milk at Dublin airport before you fly back.

FASHION & DESIGN

They don't tell you this, but Aran sweaters have only been knitted in this way in Ireland since the 19th century, with the individual pattern symbolising the life of the Irish as fishermen. Traditionally the jumpers are made from undyed, cream-coloured wool. Real Aran jumpers will set you back around 100 euros and have the name of the woman who knitted it sewn inside. Hand-woven tweedwear comes from County Donegal and enjoys a good reputation worldwide. There is a large selection of tweed jackets in muted earthy colours, in a classic cut, and visually appealing with their leather patches and leather buttons. While the tweed might appear quite rigid to start with, it moulds itself to the wearer over time and becomes more rather than less beautiful as they years go by. Magee and Harris

Aran sweaters and tweed jackets: knitwear and woven items are amongst the most popular souvenirs

are among the better-known brands. Horse riders, fishermen, hunters and golfers will also find plenty to please them in Ireland's shops; they stock a large selection of special gear and accessories.

If you're after trendy fashion and individual design, look no further than the products of the Irish family business *Avoca (www.avoca.ie)*. The range is huge: colourful ceramics, wooden and tin toys, tweed jackets in modern fashionable designs, designer clothes for women, unusual household goods and aromatic candles, as well as unmistakable cookery books, jewellery and handmade soaps, jams, chutneys and other foodstuffs. *Avoca* products are sold in high-quality shops, as well as in their own outlets (e. g. in Powerscourt House and Moll's Gap on the Ring of Kerry). The company's headquarters are the Kilmacanogue Store in Bray, County Wicklow, housed in the building once occupied by the Jameson whiskey company.

LACE & LINEN

Irish lace, made into tablecloths and handkerchiefs for instance, used to be a traditional industry in Limerick and Carrickmacross. Irish linen is known nationally for its quality and good value; you'll find it as tea towels and bed linen.

SPIRITS

One of the most popular spirits is whiskey: Paddy's and Jameson, as well, Bushmills in the North, distilled in the world's oldest distillery. Look out for the 10 or 12-year-old malts! The famous Baileys (Original Irish Cream), a liqueur (17 per cent) blended from Irish whiskey and cream, is another popular souvenir. Enjoy it as it is, with ice as a cocktail, or in coffee instead of milk or cream.

THE PERFECT ROUTE

LEISURELY STROLL THROUGH DUBLIN

The tour starts in ① *Dublin* → p. 32. The capital is best explored on foot or by boat on the River Liffey. Make sure you don't miss out on Dublin's legendary pubs. A beer in the *Temple Bar* in the hip quarter of the same name is a must. After that, repair to the roof bar of the *Guinness Storehouse* for an overview of vibrant Dublin. For glimpses of times long past, take a look at the ancient *Book of Kells* in the beautiful reading room of Trinity College Library.

CITY OF BUTTER AND BRIDGES

In two to three hours by bus or train you're in ② *Cork* → p. 46. In the Irish city with the most bridges, a worthwhile detour leads to the *Butter Museum* and the beautiful Victorian market hall, where you can partake of a *cream tea* at the *Farmgate Café*. Carry on through the pedestrian zones past Georgian townhouses and over the river to the church of Shandon (photo above). Feel free to ring their bell!

MOUNTAINS, LAKES, CASTLES

Right through the south of Ireland the train takes you to the town of ③ *Killarney* → p. 58 with its three lakes and numerous mountains. After a guided tour through *Muckross House*, a magnificent Victorian castle, enjoy your lunch in the *Muckross Garden Restaurant* – with a view of towering rhododendrons and historic greenhouses. Afterwards, why not take a stroll through ④ *Killarney National Park* → p. 58 to *Ross Castle* and a boat trip on the lake.

BEACHES AND SHEEP PASTURES

For this 124-mile drive on the spectacular coastal and panorama road of the ⑤ *Ring of Kerry* → p. 63 you're best hiring a car or joining a bus tour. You go once around the Iveragh Peninsula, past mountains and lonely beaches, with dramatic views of the raging Atlantic. The intrepid might want to brave the waves, the others can just enjoy the sight of green pastures, stately mansions and picturesque villages. A bridge leads to Valentia Island into sleepy ⑥ *Knightstown* → p. 63. Afterwards you might fancy stopping at a fish restaurant in the pretty planned town of ⑦ *Kenmare* → p. 64.

> Experience the many different faces of Ireland in a trip around most of the island – with detours to the Cliffs of Moher and Connemara

ART, CLIFFS AND LIMESTONE

From Killarney, the bus takes you to ⑧ *Limerick* → p. 67, where you can enjoy art from the Celts to the Impressionists at the *Hunt Museum* before rewarding yourself with an apple pie with cream at the in-house restaurant. In the evening, catch a medieval banquet with mead, spinet sounds and flaming torches at *Bunratty Castle*. The next day, it's time for natural attractions: for a detour to the famous ⑨ *Cliffs of Moher* → p. 75 and into the unique limestone landscape of the ⑩ *Burren* → p. 74 it's best to hire a bike or a rental car.

CITY AIR, BEACH LIFE

With its narrow lanes and historic townhouses, the vibrant university city of ⑪ *Galway* → p. 70 is the perfect place for a stroll. After some fish 'n' chips at *McDonagh's* plan your bike tour through ⑫ *Connemara* → p. 75 (photo below) with a Guinness at the *Róisín Dubh*. Don't forget your swimming togs! You'll be spreading your towel on white unspoilt beaches.

FROM DRAMATIC ISLAND SCENERY TO A CELTIC CULT SITE

Hop on the bus again, this time to ⑬ *Westport* → p. 76. At the old harbour enjoy a meal at the *Quay Cottage* fish restaurant and stroll past Georgian townhouses and the octagonal market square. If you have time, cross over to dramatic ⑭ *Achill Island* → p. 78 for some surfing or hikes through atmospheric bog and heather landscape. In ⑮ *Sligo* → p. 80, home to the great poet W B Yeats, a beer at *Hargadon's Pub* is a must, as well as a visit to the Yeats-related houses and museums. Last not least, a recommended detour to a burial site used by the Celts: climb up to megalithic ⑯ *Carrowmore* → p. 85 for its archaeological treasures, and go round the pretty lakes of the region.

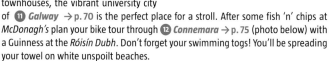

620 miles. Duration: approx. 2–3 weeks; driving time: 15–25 hours. Detailed map of the route on the back cover, in the road atlas and the pull-out map

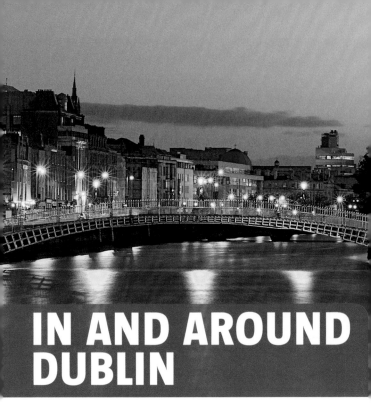

IN AND AROUND DUBLIN

Dublin and the Wicklow Mountains: in the old, eternally young capital, and the natural beauty of County Wicklow, Ireland's east boasts two magnets for tourists, aspects of the island that couldn't be more diverse.

About a million people live in and around the metropolis, nearly a quarter of the country's entire population. Street life in the alleys and streets along the Liffey shore is as lively as its young population. The public bus takes less than an hour to reach the lonely Wicklow Mountains, a fantastic hiking paradise with pretty hill landscapes and deep gorges, monastic settlements and fancy country houses. With the megalithic tomb of Newgrange, also near Dublin, the region boasts one of Europe's most impressive Stone Age burial sites.

DUBLIN

MAP INSIDE THE BACK COVER
(131 E4) *(∅ K11)* **A city is changing its image: restored façades, freshly painted entrance gates, mirrored window fronts and top-range designers – Dublin has undergone revitalisation on a grand scale.**

On chic Grafton Street the scene is still dominated by buskers, students reciting poems, newspaper sellers and school kids collecting for good causes. And in the evening, young and old meet up in one of the city's countless pubs to listen to music and chat away until the dreaded 'last orders'.

Today still, traces of the Vikings' pres-

Photo: Dublin, the River Liffey with the Halfpenny Bridge

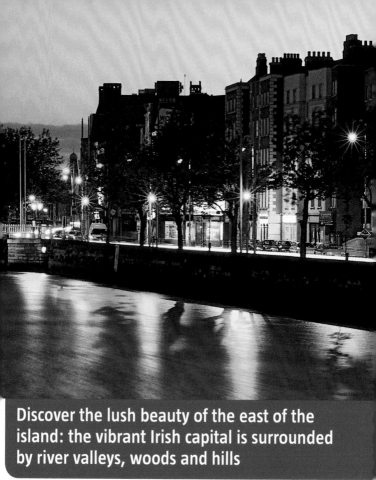

Discover the lush beauty of the east of the island: the vibrant Irish capital is surrounded by river valleys, woods and hills

🏙 **WHERE TO START?**
(U B3–4) (🗺 b3–4) Temple Bar: central quarter on the southern bank of the Liffey. From here, Trinity College, the Halfpenny Bridge leading across the river, the main shopping drag Grafton Street and the National Gallery and much more are accessible on foot. Parking: Fleet Street Car Park, access via Westmoreland Street.

ence, as the first settlers on the river Liffey, can be found in the crypt of St Audoen's church. Those are mere ruins however, hardly recognisable as former foundations. It took the Irish until 988 to conquer the Norse settlement, and then they had to hand it over again in 1170 – to the victorious Normans. Parts of the Normans' massive city wall are still visible today. A friendly invasion brought Huguenots, refugees from France, to Dublin. The contemporary urban landscape dates back to the 18th

Ancient walls: the tower of Dublin Castle belonged to a Norman fort

century, when entire rows of streets were erected in the *Georgian style* with its beautiful sash windows. A good example is *Merrion Square.* From 1855 onwards, no. 1 was home to a young Oscar Wilde (1854–1900). In 2010 Dublin was honoured with the title of 'Unesco City of Literature' – for its cultural diversity and the quality of its literary tradition then and now *(www.dublincityofliterature.ie).*

SIGHTSEEING

The excellently stocked Dublin Tourism Centre in a converted church in Suffolk Street can provide the *Dublin Tourist Trail* brochure for discovering the city's sights on foot. Various themed guided tours are available too. *Dublin Bus* run a daily hop-on-hop-off *Dublin City Tour (16 euros). 59 Upper O'Connell Street | tel. 01 7 03 30 28 | www.dublinbus.ie*

Guided walks to the beauty spots and hidden treasures of the city are available from INSIDER TIP *Pat Liddy's Walking Tours (from 5 euros | www.walkingtours. ie).* For a pretty view of the city from the river, take one of the *Liffey River Cruises (leaving from Bachelors Walk und Customs House Quay every hour from 10.30am onwards | 45 min for 14 euros | tel. 01 4 73 40 82 | www.liffeyvoyage.ie).* Historic sites are the subject of the two-hour INSIDER TIP *Historical Walking Tours of Dublin (May–Sept daily 11am and 3pm, April and Oct daily 11am, Nov–March Fri–Sun 11am | 12 euros | meeting point the front gate of*

Trinity College | www.historicalinsights. ie). Another way to discover Dublin is by pedal power. 'Dublin by bike' offers two-and-a-half- hour tours to the main sights *(daily 10.30am and 2pm from Mansion House in Dawson Street | 22 euros incl. bike and helmet | www.dub linbybike.ie)*. An audio bus tour in the footsteps of Irish rock greats such as Rory Gallagher and Bono, as well as the places where Irish authors were born or lived, is available in the shape of the INSIDER TIP *Rock 'n' Roll Writers' Bus. Wed–Sun 4 departures each | 75 min | 15 euros | Westmoreland Street | tel. 01 6 20 39 29 | www.dublinrocktour.ie* The following list only provides public transport links when the sights are located outside the city centre.

DUBLIN CASTLE (U B4) (*m b4*)

In the 13th century, the ruling Normans chose the site of a former Viking fortification to erect a fort, of which today only one tower remains. The current building dates from the 19th century. Worth seeing: the *State Apartments,* the throne room and St Patrick's Hall with its fine ceiling paintings. *Mon–Sat 10am–5pm, Sun 2–5pm | admission 4.50 euros | Dame Street | www.dublincastle.ie*

DUBLIN WRITERS MUSEUM ●
(U B2) (*m b2*)

Fine museum dedicated to writers and writing presented in a house that is a good example of an Anglo-Irish residence. The 18th-century townhouse displays a waistcoat worn by James Joyce as well as valuable first editions of Oscar Wilde's works. Panels illustrate the history of Irish literature. Dublin's writers meet next door at the *Irish Writers' Centre*. Restaurant and café. *Mon–Sat 10am–5pm, Sun 11am–5pm | admission 7.50 euros | 18 Parnell Square North | www.writersmuseum.com*

GUINNESS STOREHOUSE (0) (*m 0*)

Guinness has been brewed here in Europe's largest brewery for over 200 years. An audiovisual trail shows how it is done. Enjoy a great view from the rooftop ☀ *Gravity* Bar. *Daily 9.30am– 5pm, July/Aug to 7pm | admission 15 euros | St. James' Gate/Crane Street |*

⭐ **National Gallery**
A must for art lovers, who will find numerous masterpieces of European painting → p. 36

⭐ **Temple Bar**
Hipsters will enjoy this: in Dublin's most popular quarter, the art and pub scene rub shoulders → p. 38

⭐ **Old Library**
Order a copy of any book that was ever printed in Great Britain into the reading room → p. 38

⭐ **Monasterboice**
5th-century monastic ruins with tall High Crosses of unique beauty → p. 45

⭐ **Newgrange**
At winter solstice, the sun's rays shine into the inner chamber of this prehistoric passage tomb → p. 45

⭐ **Powerscourt Gardens**
Tea and scones on the terrace of Powerscourt House, with a superb view of the park → p. 45

www.guinnessstorehouse.com | buses 51B, 78A, 123

HALFPENNY BRIDGE ☼ (U B3) (📖 b3)

This small pedestrian bridge appears in most Dublin holiday shots. For centuries, boats and ferries took Dubliners across the Liffey. In the 19th century, life became easier when a metal bridge over the river was financed with a half-penny toll per crossing. Today it's free. *City centre west of O'Connell Bridge*

JAMES JOYCE CENTRE (U B2) (📖 b2)

James Joyce (1882–1941) wrote only a few books, but those proved a major influence on the literature of the 20th century – not least his most famous novel, Ulysses, telling the events of a single day

Poet with hat: Joyce statue in Earl Street North

– the 16th of June *(Bloomsday)*. This 18th-century Georgian townhouse is dedicated to Joyce's memory, housing the James Joyce cultural centre with exhibitions and the Ulysses Café. Guided tours to places associated with Joyce are also available *(10 euros). Tue–Sat 10am–5pm | admission 5 euros | 35 North Great George's Street | www.jamesjoyce.ie*

LIFFEY BOARD WALK (U B3) (📖 b3)

A wooden boardwalk leading along the Liffey's northern bank from O'Connell Bridge to Halfpenny Bridge, ideal for a leisurely stroll. Part of the riverbank (at Lower Ormond Quay) was converted into an  INSIDER TIP ▶ *Italian Quarter* (also known as Quartier Bloom) with Italian restaurants and nice shops.

NATIONAL GALLERY ★ ● (U C4) (📖 c4)

An oasis of calm and a journey into the world of high art: works by Jack B Yeats, Ireland's most important 20th-century artist, as well as a Caravaggio recently discovered in Dublin are amongst the gems of this collection of European art. Workshops and free guided tours by art students, concerts and special exhibitions. *Mon–Wed, Fri/Sat 9.30am–5.30pm, Thu 9.30am–8.30pm, Sun 12 noon–5.30pm | free admission | Merrion Square West, next to Leinster House | www.nationalgallery.ie*

OLD JAMESON DISTILLERY (U A3) (📖 a3)

Since the worldwide successful whiskey brand moved production to Midleton (near Cork), the distillery, built in 1790, only houses a show distillery. Still, on a INSIDER TIP ▶ guided tour (incl. a drink) you will hear how the 'water of life' is produced. *Daily 9.30am–5.30pm | admission 14 euros, whiskey tasting: 8 euros,*

Check out the Caravaggio and much more: the National Gallery shows European art

premium whiskey tasting: 22.50 euros | Bow Street, Smithfield Village | www.jamesonwhiskey.com

ROYAL HOSPITAL ● (0) (𝄪 0)

Built in the 17th century as a military pensioners' home, the building today serves as a *National Centre for Culture and the Arts* with exhibitions, concerts, theatre and cultural events of all kinds. It also houses the excellent *IMMA*, the *Irish Museum of Modern Art (www.imma.ie)*. *Tue–Sat 10am–5.30pm, Sun 12 noon–5.30 pm | free admission | Military Road Kilmainham | www.rhk.ie | buses 26, 51, 51B, 78A, 79, 90, 123*

INSIDER TIP ▶ SMITHFIELD VILLAGE
(U A3) (𝄪 a3)

The restored block north of the Liffey is following the path of Temple Bar to become a second hip district. Several arts institutions are housed here, also restaurants and bars, a hotel, the *Old Jameson Distillery (1780, see above)* and as a special attraction an ⚘ industrial chimney converted into a viewing tower. *Between Bow and Smithfield Street, west of O'Connell Street*

ST PATRICK'S CATHEDRAL
(U A4–5) (𝄪 a4–5)

Ireland's largest cathedral was erected on the ruins of a Norman church. The 18th-century writer Jonathan Swift, famous for his satirical Gulliver's Travels, was dean here for 30 years. Swift's grave is located at the southwest entrance. *Mon–Sat 9am–5pm, Sun 9–11am and 12.30–3pm, 4.30–6.30pm | admission 5.50 euros | www.stpatrickscathedral.ie | St Patrick's Close*

DUBLIN

TEMPLE BAR ★ (U B3) (⑭ b3)

In Dublin's hip quarter you can experience street art and rock music, browse alternative and long-established shops or quirky boutiques, enjoy French haute cuisine or try out trendy bars and restaurants. The true treasure of Temple Bar – which on weekend nights is sadly overrun with tourists and drunken stag parties – are its cultural sites: the *Irish Film Centre* (showing classic movies and small Irish productions), the *Gallery of Photography* (photo exhibitions and workshops) and the *Temple Bar Gallery* (where dozens of artists show their work), and the *Projects Arts Centre* avant-garde stage which welcomes exciting productions. Get hold of a detailed map and a sightseeing pass (including a map, discounts and a list of members) at the *Information Centre (East Essex Street 12 | tel. 01 6772255 | www.templebar.ie). Between Westmoreland and Fishamble Street, southeast of Halfpenny Bridge*

THE SPIRE (U B3) (⑭ b3)

When erected in 2003, the 393-ft steel needle, measuring 3 m at its base and 15 cm at the top, became the city's highest monument and its new landmark. Illuminated at night, it sways by up to 1.5 m – a spectacular sight! *O'Connell St., next to the GPO central post office*

TRINITY COLLEGE LIBRARY
(U C4) (⑭ c4)

Founded in 1592, Ireland's most renowned university is situated right at the heart of the city centre and charms visitors with its splendid Georgian buildings, nestling in a landscaped park. Amongst the university's eight libraries is the ★ *Old Library,* built between 1712 and 1732, which attracts the most visitors. In the *Long Room,* a 70 m-long reading room with wooden vaulted roof, shutters protect the 200,000 oldest of the 4.5 million books in the College's collection from the sun. The exhibits of

Reading room in the Old Library: hundreds of thousands of precious books are here

the impressive reading room include a rare copy of the Easter proclamation of the Irish Republic of 1916. Here you'll also find the *Book of Kells* gospel. Boasting extraordinary illumination, the Latin manuscript was probably made around the year 800 by monks and since its restoration (1953) has been exhibited in four volumes. Two of the overall 680 pages are on show every day. *Daily 9.30am–5pm | admission 9 euros | between Nassau and Pearse Street, entrance in College Street | www.tcd.ie/library*

FOOD & DRINK

A 2.5-hour guided tour of markets and shops with tastings *(Dublin Tasting Trail)* is an excellent stand-in for lunch *(for exact times and place: tel. 01 4 97 12 45 | 45 euros | www.fabulousfoodtrails.com).*

BEWLEY'S ORIENTAL CAFE (U B4) (*b4*)
Still the iconic meeting place in Dublin, serving coffees and teas as well as pasta and salads in an Art Nouveau interior since 1927. *Daily | 78/79 Grafton Street | tel. 01 6 72 77 19 | www.bewleys.com | Moderate*

CHAPTER ONE (U B2) (*b2*)
Head chef Ross Lewis' creations, beautifully fusing haute cuisine and rustic Irish fare, earned him a Michelin star. This makes the *lunch menu* for 30 euros and the 37.50-euro *pre-theatre menu* (served before 7pm) a real bargain. *Tue–Sat | 18–19 Parnell Square North | tel. 01 8 73 22 66 | www.chapteronerestaurant.com | Expensive*

COPPINGER ROW (U B4) (*b4*)
Young scene, fresh, Mediterranean cuisine: Moroccan lentil soup with chick-peas and lamb, tuna with aubergine; in good weather also outside seating. Water for refills is available for 1 euro, of which 50 cent goes to cancer research. *Tue–Sun | 48 Coppinger Row, off South William Street | tel. 01 6 72 98 84 | www.coppingerrow.com | Moderate*

INSIDER TIP GOVINDA'S (U B3) (*b3*)
Delicious vegetarian dishes: eat well and inexpensively in the restaurant of the spiritually inspired Kirtan Centre (yoga and meditation available too) in the centre of Dublin. *Daily | 83 Middle Abbey Street | tel. 01 4 75 03 09 | www.govindas.ie | Budget*

JACOB'S LADDER (U C4) (*c4*)
Creative cuisine, served in several rooms, with mussels a house speciality. *Tue–Sat | 4–5 Nassau Street | tel. 01 6 70 38 65 | Expensive*

KANUM (U C6) (*c6*)
This small restaurant and takeaway serves delicious Thai dishes for little money. A must: the coconut soup with lemongrass and chicken, and the tiger prawns with ginger and lots of spicy sauces. *Daily | 77 Mespil Road | tel. 01 6 60 86 16 | www.kanum.ie | Budget*

RHODES D7 (U B3) (*b3*)
English TV chef Gary Rhodes runs a bistro here serving modern cuisine – his potato salads are legend! *Tue–Sat | Mary's Abbey | tel. 01 8 04 44 44 | Moderate*

TROCADERO (U B4) (*b4*)
Theatre restaurant with hip clientele, serving a good-value INSIDER TIP early-bird menu from 5 to 7pm. *Mon–Sat | 4 St Andrew Street | tel. 01 6 77 55 45 | www.trocadero.ie | Expensive*

SHOPPING

Dublin's main shopping drags are Grafton Street and the cheaper O'Connell Street and Henry Street. Dodge any rain showers with a stroll through the indoor *shopping malls* at St Stephen's Green. Also pleasant: the ● *Powerscourt Centre*: boutiques and cafés stretching along a glass-roofed inner courtyard, as well as the *Westbury Shopping Mall,* both located near Grafton Street.

BROWN THOMAS (U B4) (*ω b4*)
Founded in 1849, this department store stocks everything that's fancy, expensive and currently hip: from Hunter wellies via Stella McCartney's design creations to perfume by Jo Malone. Look out for the sales in January and July, when items are reduced up to 60 per cent. *88–95 Grafton Street*

EASON HANNA'S (U C4) (*ω c4*)
Long-established Irish bookshop stocking titles by nearly all Irish authors, plus antiquarian books. *1 Dawson Street*

FALLON & BYRNE (U B4) (*ω b4*)
Trendy gourmet trio across three storeys: market-fresh groceries are sold in the food hall in light, contemporary design, there is an organic restaurant and a large wine cellar. *11–17 Exchequer Street | www.fallonandbyrne.com*

KILKENNY SHOP (U C4) (*ω c4*)
The go-to place for everything and anything that is billed as typically Irish: ceramics in earthy colours, waxed raincoats, tweed scarves and jackets, cashmere and lambswool jumpers, linen, lace and woodcarvings. Not cheap but of the highest quality. *5/6 Nassau Street | www.kilkennyshop.com*

INSIDER TIP MOORE STREET MARKET (U B3) (*ω b3*)
A reminder of Old Dublin: various street stalls selling fruit and veg, as well as flowers; some of the wares are still delivered by horse and cart. *Mon–Sat 9am–1pm | Moore Street*

INSIDER TIP RORY'S FISHING TACKLE (U B3) (*ω b3*)
An institution: Rory, a friendly businessman and fisherman, sells everything anglers need: from live bait to willow baskets. *17A Temple Bar | www.rorys.ie*

Colourful shopping in Grafton Street

ENTERTAINMENT

ABBEY THEATRE (U C3) (𝄞 c3)

Today's national theatre, founded in 1904 by William Butler Yeats, regularly showcases Irish authors (classics and modern). *26 Lower Abbey Street | tel. 01 8 78 72 22 | www.abbeytheatre.ie*

THE BRAZEN HEAD (U A3) (𝄞 a3)

The city's oldest pub dates back to 1198. Daily live music quickly fills up the three rooms. The courtyard is much in demand in summer, in winter it's a meeting place for the smokers. *20 Lower Bridge Street | www.brazenhead.com*

DUBLIN LITERARY PUB CRAWL ●
(U B4) (𝄞 b4)

The Dublin Literary Pub Crawl promises a boozy literary evening – and delivers. Led by actors, walk in the footsteps of famous Irish poets and philosophers – starting from the premise that a lot of Irish literature is owed to the pub. Tickets are available from the Dublin Tourism Centre and at *The Duke*. Try and avoid Friday and Saturday evenings when the pubs are crammed. *Meeting point April–Oct daily 7.30pm, Nov–March Thu–Sun 7.30pm at The Duke's | 9 Duke Street | 12 euros | www.dublinpubcrawl.com*

FITZSIMON'S (U B3) (𝄞 b3)

The restaurant serves rustic Irish fare, the popular bar plays *traditional music*. There are also Irish folkdance workshops, at weekends in the afternoon and on Sunday mornings: excellent fun! *21–22 Wellington Quay Temple Bar | tel. 01 6 77 93 15 | www.fitzsimonshotel.com*

THE MUSICAL BUS (U B3) (𝄞 b3)

A bus trip taking in three pubs with live music. Tickets from the Tourism Centre. *Fri/Sat 8pm | starting point Suffolk Street*

Centuries of pub culture:
the bar of The Brazen Head

Bus Stop | 22 euros | tel. 01 4 75 33 13 | www.discoverdublin.ie/musicalbus.htm

INSIDER TIP ▶ MUSICAL PUB CRAWL ●
(U B3) (𝄞 b3)

Fancy listening to some pipes, fiddle and the box? At this two-and-a-half pub crawl two professional musicians lead you through the vibrant pubs of the Temple Bar quarter. Along the way they play some music and tell the history of Irish music. *Start April–Oct daily 7.30pm, Nov–March Tue–Sat 7.30pm at Hotel Oliver St John Gogarty's | Anglesea Street | 12 euros | tel. 01 4 75 33 13 | www. discoverdublin.ie/musicalpubcrawl. html*

THE NATIONAL CONCERT HALL
(U B–C5) (𝄞 b–c5)

The home of the National Symphony Orchestra of Ireland presents top classical and light music. *Earlsfort Terrace, near St Stephen's Green | tel. 01 4 17 00 77 | www. nch.ie*

DUBLIN

O'DONOGHUE'S (U C5) (*c5*)
The cradle of the 'Dubliners' band, with impressive pictures on the walls, always packed. *15 Merrion Row | tel. 01 6 60 71 94 | www.odonoghues.ie*

names. *Curved Street, Temple Bar | tel. 01 6 70 92 02 | www.tbmc.ie*

WHELAN'S (U B3) (*b3*)
Daily changing programme with cur-

Lovers of live music will come away happy every night: Temple Bar

PRAVDA (U B3) (*b3*)
This huge pub is decorated with symbols of bolshevism; punters ranging from hippies and left-leaning liberals to chic types enjoy the vast range of available vodkas. *35 Lower Liffey Street at the Halfpenny Bridge | www.pravda.ie*

PROJECT ARTS CENTRE (U B3) (*b 3*)
Rock concerts, avant-garde productions and modern dance are on offer at this arts centre in hip Temple Bar; arts exhibitions in the lobby. *39 East Essex Street | Temple Bar | tel. 01 8 81 96 13 | www.project.ie*

THE TEMPLE BAR MUSIC CENTRE (U B3) (*b3*)
Rock, underground, crossover – daily live music by newcomers and big Irish

rent pop and rock bands. *25 Wexford St. | tel. 01 4 78 07 66 | www.whelanslive.com*

WHERE TO STAY

AVALON HOUSE (U B4) (*b4*)
This Victorian guesthouse has a central location and offers a good number of dorms, but also single and double rooms, as well as several communal spaces. Internet access is by coin-operated machines. The price includes a *continental breakfast*. Café/restaurant. *71 rooms with 281 beds | 55 Aungier Street | tel. 01 4 75 00 01 | www.avalon-house.ie | Budget*

BLOOMS HOTEL (U B3) (𝄙 b3)
Comfortable rooms right in the thick of things, with an in-house pub, live music and nightclub. *86 rooms | Anglesea Street | Temple Bar | tel. 01 6 71 56 22 | www.blooms.ie | Moderate*

THE DYLAN (U B4) (𝄙 b4)
Discreet luxury in an award-winning boutique hotel boasting large rooms and marble-clad bathrooms with underfloor heating. Mediterranean-inspired courtyard. *44 rooms | Eastmoreland Place | tel. 01 6 60 30 00 | www.dylan.ie | Expensive*

GRAND CANAL HOTEL (0) (𝄙 O)
Modern hotel in the well-heeled Ballsbridge part of town (opposite the DART local train station). *142 rooms | Upper Grand Canal Street | tel. 01 6 46 10 00 | www.grandcanalhotel.com | Moderate*

KINLAY HOUSE (U B5) (𝄙 b5)
Victorian hostel offering comfortable double rooms alongside traditional dorms. *33 rooms | 2–12 Lord Edward St. | tel. 01 6 79 66 44 | www.kinlayhouse.ie | Budget*

INFORMATION

DUBLIN TOURISM CENTRE (U B4) (𝄙 b4)
St Andrew's Church | Suffolk Street | tel. (*) 1850 23 03 30 | www.visitdublin.com
Additional offices at the airport, in Dun Laoghaire port, at 14 O'Connell Street and Baggot Street Bridge.
If you are planning on doing a lot of sightseeing, it is worth picking up a *Dublin Pass* right on arrival at Dublin airport. The pass is valid for one or several days (from 35 euros) and offers free admission to 31 attractions alongside a free bus transfer into the city centre *(www.dublinpass.ie)*. The Freedom of the City of Dublin pass includes the Airlink bus from the airport into the city centre, the hop-on-hop-off Dublin Bus Tour and all buses in Dublin for 3 days (72 hours). You can buy this for 25 euros from Dublin Tourism and the Airlink ticket machine at the airport.

WHERE TO GO

DUN LAOGHAIRE (131 E4) (𝄙 K11)
The fast DART suburban train brings you to the port town (pop. 60,000) just under 7 miles south of the city. There are great views of Dublin Bay from here, especially on a stroll along the eastern ⚓ harbour walls. Catch a glimpse of Celtic symbols in the oratory at the *Dominican convent (Lower George's Street)*.

GLENDALOUGH ⚓
(131 E5) (𝄙 J12)
Only 30 miles south of Dublin, a unique hiking and natural paradise awaits: nu-

LOW BUDGET

▶ The *An Oige Hostel* is a cheap alternative to a hotel. *364 beds | 61 Mountjoy Street | tel. 01 8 30 45 55 | www.anoige.ie | buses 41A, 16A*

▶ ● Second-hand wares and markets; every weekend in the Temple Bar quarter: *Cow's Lane Fashion Market, Cow's Lane (Sat) | Temple Bar Food Market, Meeting House Square (Sat) | Temple Bar Book Market, Temple Bar Square (Sat/Sun; 10am–5.30pm)*

▶ The *Rambler Ticket* for Dublin's buses (including the bus from and to the airport) is particularly good value: *1 day/6 euros; 3 days/13.30 euros; 5 days/20 euros. Available from the airport and in many shops.*

merous routes taking several days, between 37 and 62 miles, lead through the hilly country of the *Wicklow Mountains*. Amongst the highlights of this area, the narrow valley of Glendalough encompasses two green shimmering lakes, framed by mountains. ● Founded in the 7th century by Saint Kevin, the monastery of the same name soon became the spiritual centre of Ireland. From the 9th century onwards, the round tower, 108 ft high, a refuge for the monks during Viking attacks, stood at the heart of the monastic town *(admission 3 euros | www.glendalough.ie)*. Nature lovers should take the *Falcon Trail*, a 2.5-mile hiking trail, at the Upper Lake.

KILDARE (130 C5) (*∅ H12*)

The town (pop. 4200) featuring 18th-century houses lies 30 miles west of Dublin (on the N 7) in the heart of the Irish horse country. The *cathedral* (1875) stands on the remains of a monastery said to have been founded in 470 by Saint Brigid – for both nuns and monks. It is here that this important saint, highly revered in Ireland (St Brigid's Day is 1 February) is said to have kept a holy fire burning day and night, keeping up a pre-Christian tradition. Today's building however only incorporates parts from the 13th century. A round tower dating back to the 12th century stands next to the church, and the church holds some medieval tombstones. Consider visiting the National Stud in Tully *(www.irish-national-stud.ie)* a good 3 miles east of town.

KILLINEY (131 E4) (*∅ K12*)

This pretty coastal town (7.5 miles southeast) is home to several Irish rock stars. Standing on a hill in Victoria Road, the neo-gothic *Ayesha Castle* belongs to the Irish singer Enya, who renamed it Manderley Castle. Take a stroll in the surrounding hill country, to Dalkey for instance, for the prettiest views of Killiney Bay and Dublin.

Amidst a peaceful landscape: the round tower of Glendalough, once a refuge for monks

MONASTERBOICE ★ ●
(131 E2) (*⚲ J10*)

It is well worth driving the 7.5 miles north of Dublin to the remains of a monastery probably founded in the 5th century and boasting Ireland's most ornate High Crosses, amongst them the beautifully ornate *Muiredach's Cross*. Carved into stone, the representations tell biblical stories. The complex also features a round tower, two 13th-century churches, two tomb slabs and a still functional old sundial. *www.monasterboice.net*

NEWGRANGE ★ ●
(131 D2–3) (*⚲ J10*)

Some 5000 years old, the burial chamber 36 miles northwest of Dublin is a wonder of early architecture; the entire complex, with Knowth and Dowth (the latter not accessible to the public) is a Unesco World Heritage site. The interior of the megalithic burial mound, some 75 m long and 13 m high, can only be entered through a narrow passage 18 m long. Above the entrance is an opening through which the sun reaches the burial chamber, bathing it in light on five days, around 21 December, at winter solstice. It is said that the stones at those times appear as if dipped in gold. *In summer 9am–7pm, in winter 10am–5pm | admission by guided tour only, every half-hour | admission 6 euros | www.newgrange. com | bookings at the Visitors' Centre on the L 21 | 1.2 mi west of Donore*

A shuttle bus leaves daily at 8.45 und 11.15am from the Tourist Information in Suffolk Street and 15 minutes later from O'Connell Street (Royal Dublin Hotel) for Newgrange (returning 1 and 4pm, 18 euros return).

POWERSCOURT GARDENS ★ ●
(131 E5) (*⚲ K12*)

Powerscourt Gardens is considered one of Ireland's most beautiful landscaped parks. The complex consists of the imposing *Powerscourt Estate* manor house and the extensive green spaces around it, including a Japanese garden and a pet cemetery. Visit the castle park as well as the waterfall *(3 mi),* and enjoy the superb natural backdrop from the refined café terrace. Next door, the small maze of the INSIDER TIP *Avoca Store* in *Powerscourt House* is a treasure trove for anybody looking for colourful imaginative gifts. *Daily 9.30am–5.30pm | admission 8 euros, waterfall 5 euros | www. powerscourt.ie | Enniskerry (11 mi south of Dublin) | bus 44c from Townsend Street, Dublin 2 or bus 185 from Bray*

Next to Powerscourt Gardens, the Ritz Carlton Powerscourt is a palatial hotel in the Palladian style with a fantastic spa, 36-hole golf course and ☀ a luxury suites with fabulous views of the Sugarloaf Mountains. *200 rooms | Enniskerry | tel. 01 2 74 88 88 | www.ritzcarlton.com | Expensive*

THE SOUTH

Picture-postcard Ireland: if one region comes close to the cliché of an intact world with charming landscape, picturesque villages and dramatic coastline, it's the south. Turn literally any corner and a new highlight is revealed.

Cork too, the country's second-largest city, gives an impression of good spirits and wealth. Numerous fishing villages nearby look so trim and picturesque that you want to stay for ever. In Beara, Iveragh and Dingle, peninsulas popular with Irish visitors too poke out into the Atlantic. Try to go around at least one of them by car – and you will fall for their beauty, guaranteed. More small islands, and very interesting ones at that – such as the Blaskets – lie off the coast. Stretching out towards the north, the un-

dulating and fertile hills of Co. Limerick, predominantly used for agriculture, are scattered with small towns from Norman times and picturesque river valleys.

CORK

MAP INSIDE THE BACK COVER
(134 A5) (*M E16*) There's a downright pleasant air about the country's second-largest city (pop. 190,000) with its many bridges across the river Lee. You will see plenty of students of UCC (University College Cork) studying or relaxing in the street cafés in front of Georgian façades.

A number of excellent restaurants are within easy walking distance, as well as

A rocky coastline and hidden coves:
the fishing villages of the south boast
colourful houses – and pubs ...

CITY **WHERE TO START?**

St Patrick's Street: branching off from this shopping street are various pedestrian zones with beautifully restored Georgian houses. St Patrick's Bridge leads across the River Lee into the northern parts of the city. The bus station and a multi-storey car park are on the other side of the river, at the eastern end of Merchant's Quay.

many pubs and shops. Corkonians are experts in the art of the good life – and also in spending lot of money. Just check out the long queues at the cashpoints.

The name Cork derives from the Gaelic Corcaigh, meaning marsh or boggy terrain. The city stretches out across an island amidst the river Lee, which splits into two arms here. These days 25 bridges lead across the river, while many of today's roads used to be waterways; even the main shopping drag of St Patrick's Street was still serving as moorings for cargo ships in 1750.

The Crawford Art Gallery in the morning – schoolchildren contemplating the works of art

There has been a known settlement here since the Middle Ages, with St Finbarr founding his monastic school around the year 650. However, the only building that remains from this time, Red Abbey, was outside the town. During the siege of Cork by the English the city wall was destroyed in its entirety in 1690; some foundations are still visible near the entrance arch in Bishop Lucey Park and in the Grand Parade Hotel.

With the 19th-century establishment of the butter market, today situated on Shandon Hill, trade with Spain, Holland, Germany, North America and the West Indies was given a substantial boost. Magnificent Georgian and Victorian townhouses are a reminder of the wealth of the time.

SIGHTSEEING

CITY HALL

Though the city hall on the river Lee was only built in 1936 from limestone, it fits in very well into the surrounding historic urban architecture. *Albert Quay/ Anglesea Street*

CORK BUTTER MUSEUM

The *Butter Market* is a living illustration of 19th-century dairy farming, butter production and trade – all the way to today's famous Kerrygold brand. *March–Oct daily 10am–5pm, July/Aug 10am–6pm | admission 4 euros | Exchange St., O'Connell Square | www.corkbutter.museum*

CORK CITY GAOL

What looks like more of a palace from the outside, is a prison used by the British from 1824 onwards for 100 years, mainly for political prisoners. Today the building houses an impressive museum. Walk through the old cells, accompanied by the odd sound effect added over the loudspeaker. Afterwards, why not partake of the *prisoner menu* in the café? *March–Oct daily 9.30am–5pm, Nov–Feb 10am–4pm | admission 7 euros | from Sunday's Well Road, Convent Avenue | www.corkcitygaol.com*

CORK PUBLIC MUSEUM

The history of the city, from its Early Christian beginnings to the early 20th-century revolt against the English, is told in a splendid Georgian house. Particularly interesting are the documents about the uprising against the British and the exhibition on the Irish freedom movement from the Easter Rising 1916 onwards. *Mon–Fri 11am–1pm and 2–5pm, Sat to 4pm | free admission | Mardyke Walk (Fitzgerald Park)*

COURT HOUSE

Architecturally, this is a mixed bag: the courthouse with its imposing entrance façade of Corinthian columns was erected in 1835. Its rear is faithful to Tudor style, while the splendid exterior is complemented by an interior clad in red and green marble. *Washington Street*

CRAWFORD ART GALLERY ●

In the morning, you're likely to have this art gallery, erected in 1724 as a customs house, all to yourself. The building to-day houses works by Old Masters and modern Irish artists, as well as replicas of statues from antiquity. There's good-value café-restaurant too. *Mon–Sat 10am–5pm, Thu to 8pm | admission free | Emmet Place | www.crawfordartgallery.com*

FITZGERALD PARK

Lying between Western Road and the Lee (access from Mardyke Walk), the green heart of Cork boasts various entertainment options, fine sculptures, the city museum and a reasonably priced café.

GRAND PARADE

The broad street that today forms the backbone of the city used to be a canal and is limited by the southern arm of the river Lee, by the City Market and Bishop Lucey Park. The park has remnants of the old city wall, and the entrance gate, which used to lead to the grain market, dates from the year 1850. At its southern end, the Grand Parade is overlooked by

---

⭐ **Skellig Michael**
The summit of the 712-ft high, pyramid-shaped rock island is occupied by an Early Christian ecclesiastical complex → p. 64

⭐ **Cork City Market**
A piece of England on the Emerald Isle: discover impressive arches, fountains and galleries in the Victorian halls → p. 52

⭐ **Blarney Castle**
Stronghold boasting a mythical stone that even Sir Walter Scott kissed back in the day → p. 55

⭐ **Youghal**
Pretty harbour town with historic city wall → p. 58

⭐ **Muckross House**
Splendid Victorian manor house at the heart of a national park → p. 59

⭐ **Ring of Kerry**
Coastal panorama road in arguably the most beautiful part of Ireland → p. 63

⭐ **Kinsale**
Timbered buildings, forts and fresh fish → p. 64

MARCO POLO HIGHLIGHTS

the *National Monument*. This was erected for four rebels who fell fighting against the British between 1798 and 1867.

RED ABBEY

The square tower forms part of a former medieval Augustinian monastery, making it the oldest building in town. *Red Abbey Street*

SHANDON CHURCH & BELLS ⚆

Visible from afar, St Anne's church atop a hill north of the river Lee was built in 1722. One peculiarity is the weathervane in the shape of a salmon, with a 3 m span. For a fee, the famous *glockenspiel*

650. Designed in the Gothic style by architect William Burgess, the church with its 131-ft tower was consecrated in 1870. Watch out for the marble work inside, the window rose in the west front and the numerous sculptures. A golden angel holding two trumpets to its mouth sits enthroned above the eastern side. *Mon–Sat 10am–5pm | between Dean and Bishop Street | www.cathedral.cork. anglican.org*

ST PATRICK'S BRIDGE

After several bridges across the river Lee had been destroyed by flooding, the current bridge at the northern end of

Vista of Cork with the towers of St Finbarr's Cathedral

can be set to work. *Mon–Sat 10am–4pm | admission 6 euros | Shandon Street | www.shandonbells.org*

ST FINBARR'S CATHEDRAL

St Finbarr is said to have founded a monastery on the site of this church around

the main shopping drag of St Patrick's Street was constructed from limestone. Boasting a perfectly worked balustrade and three beautifully curved arches, this is a true beauty of a bridge. *Bridge Street*

TRISKEL ARTS CENTRE

The site behind Christ Church puts on exhibitions, music and theatre, as well as INSIDER TIP readings in English and Gaelic (bilingual). Café. *Tue–Sat 10am–5pm | Tobin Street between South Main Street and Grand Parade | tel. 021 4 27 20 22 | www.triskelart.com*

UNIVERSITY COLLEGE CORK

Founded in 1845, the university is Ireland's leading research institution. The campus boasts buildings in the Tudor Gothic style (the central *quadrangle* in particular) as well as the *Honan Chapel* and its lead windows. On Mon, Wed, Fri and Sat at 3pm the visitors' centre in the Stone Corridor of the North Wing *(tel. 021 4 90 18 76)* offers INSIDER TIP one-hour guided tours *(4 euros). Main entrance Western Road, corner of Donovan's Road | www.ucc.ie*

FOOD & DRINK

INSIDER TIP BOQUERIA

Ireland goes Spain: delicious Spanish tapas in a restyled traditional pub. Particularly tasty are the *piquillos* (red peppers filled with goat's cheese and almonds), imported salami and chorizo. *16 Bridge Street | tel. 021 4 55 90 49 | www.boqueria.ie | Moderate–Expensive*

INSIDER TIP CAFÉ PARADISO

Bistro serving top vegetarian fare. New Zealand-influenced chef Denis Cotter is considered a creative genius when it comes to green spelt and chard. *Tue–Sat | 16 Lancaster Quay, corner of Western Road | tel. 021 4 27 79 39 | www.cafeparadiso.ie | Expensive*

EASTERN TANDOORI

Award-winning Indian cuisine in a fine and refined atmosphere, also open for lunch. *1/2 Emmet Place | tel. 021 4 27 20 20 | Moderate*

THE FARMGATE CAFÉ

Meeting place on the gallery of the *English Food Market*. Specialities: fish and poultry, as well as Irish cheeses. *Mon–Sat | Princess Street | tel. 021 4 27 81 34 | www.farmgate.ie | Budget*

FOUR LIARS BISTRO

Good pit-stop for a cocktail or a light dinner before hitting the town: chicken in a sauce of forest mushrooms and potato-salmon paté are among the classics served here. *Butter Exchange, Shandon | tel. 021 4 39 40 40 | www.fourliarsbistro.com | Moderate*

JACOBS ON THE MALL

Modern purist design in a historic building (former Turkish baths), ambitious contemporary cuisine combining Irish cooking traditions with international influences. Unpretentious for lunch, stylish and refined for dinner. One choice for afters never disappoints: butterscotch pudding. *Mon–Sat | 30A South Mall | tel. 021 4 25 15 30 | www.jacobsonthemall.com | Moderate*

JACQUES

Number one in town: Jacques has been committed to excellent French cooking for over 25 years. Much recommended are the three-course changing menus *(35 euros | Thu–Sat).* Best book a table. *Mon–Sat | 9 Phoenix Street near the main post office | tel. 021 4 27 73 87 | www.jacquesrestaurant.ie | Expensive*

QUAY CO-OP ☺

Founded in 1982, a stalwart of the formerly alternative scene, this restaurant serves vegetarian dishes such as pizza, lasagne, soups, salads and vegetables from organic agriculture that you pick up yourself at the counter. An organic bakery and a grocery form part of the venture too. *Mon–Sat | 24 Sullivan's Quay | tel. 021 4 31 70 26 | www.quaycoop.com | Budget*

are also available, as well as all different kinds of fish from the region and a large selection of mussels. *Mon–Sat 9am–5pm | Victorian halls in the centre, between Grand Parade and St Patrick's Street (Princes Street)*

SHOPPING

COAL QUAY MARKET

Second-hand goods from hats to shoes, also fresh and new items ranging from a head of cabbage to CDs: all this is on offer in historic halls, at street stalls, in tiny shops as well as by flying vendors. *Sat 9am–5pm | Cornmarket Street*

CORK CITY MARKET ★ ☺

With its architecture of arches, fountains and galleries, the attractive market complex built in 1786 in the city centre is also called the *English Market*. Fruit and veg come from organic agriculture, poultry and meat from organic farms. Daily fresh salmon, langoustines and lobster

MERCHANT'S QUAY

Numerous boutiques, department stores, cafés, music stores and other shops are housed in a skilfully restored warehouse on the river. The first floor has a self-service restaurant with café, a meeting place mostly for locals. The Dunnes and Roches Store department stores are right next door. *St Patrick's Bridge | www.merchantsquaycork.com*

ENTERTAINMENT

AN BODHRÁN

Pub with stylish old-fashioned interior. Live music five times a week. *42 Oliver Plunkett Street*

Cork City Market is housed in Victorian halls

AN SPAILPIN FANAC

Busy, cosy pub, with near-daily traditional music. At weekends in particular, students and tourists come together here. *28/29 South Main Street*

CORK OPERA HOUSE

A glass building filled with culture: the programme features opera, theatre and dance, but also musicals, revues, children's theatre and comedy. *Emmet Place | tel. 021 4 27 00 22 | www.corkoperahouse.ie*

DAN LOWREY'S

Classy and stylish Irish pub with English elegance; pretty glass décor, fancy furnishings. *13 MacCurtain Street*

EVERYMAN PALACE THEATRE

The resident ensemble puts on mostly modern and classic Irish plays. *15 MacCurtain Street | tel. 021 4 50 16 73 | www. everymanpalace.com*

FRED ZEPPELINS

'Keep on rocking in the free world!' is the motto they follow at 'Fredz', including live music. *8 Parliament Street off South Mall | www.fredscork.com*

INSIDERTIP ▶ THE MUTTON LANE INN

In the city's oldest (1787) and most beautiful pub – if a bit dingy and with an alternative touch – you can do more than just have a pint. The place puts on exhibitions of local artists and jam sessions on a Monday. *3 Mutton Lane, off St Patrick's St. (next to English Market)*

SIN È

In this popular traditional pub – the Irish means 'That's it' – there is live music on Fridays and Sundays (6.30pm) as well as on Tuesdays (from 9.30pm). *8 Coburg Street | www.peoplesrepublicofcork. com/SinE*

WHERE TO STAY

CORK INTERNATIONAL HOSTEL

Large Victorian brick house near the university and Fitzgerald Park; the city centre is just over a mile's walk. *96 beds | 1/2 Redclyffe, Western Road | tel. 021 4 54 32 89 | www.anoige.ie | Budget*

GARNISH HOUSE

Pretty *bed & breakfast* accommodation opposite the university and near Fitzgerald Park, pleasant atmosphere and reliable service. Close to the centre. *14 rooms | Western Road, corner of Donovan's Road | tel. 021 4 27 5111 | www. garnish.ie | Moderate*

HAYFIELD MANOR

Living like the Irish landed gentry: located just over a mile outside the city centre in a park, the manor house spoils its guests with exquisitely designed rooms, several excellent restaurants and a spa with outdoor jacuzzi. Sophisticated touches include the lavish five-o'clock tea and sherry in the library. *88 rooms | Perrott Avenue, College Road | tel. 021 4 84 95 00 | www.hayfieldmanor.ie | Expensive*

KILLARNEY GUEST HOUSE

Charming house dating back to 1847, yet all rooms en-suite, very comfortable and friendly. Parking available. *19 rooms | Western Road opposite the university | tel. 021 4 27 02 90 | www.killarneyguesthouse. com | Moderate*

KINLAY HOUSE

This hostel offers not only dorms, but also double rooms with en-suite facilities. Free breakfast up to 9.30am, 24-hour service, kitchen, phone, internet access. Plus extras such as laundry service and bike storage. *104 beds | Bob and Joan*

CORK

Walk Shandon | tel. 021 4 50 89 66 | www.kinlayhouse.ie | Budget

INSIDER TIP MALDRON

Housed in a Georgian building, this town hotel has modern rooms and a generous wellness area, boasting steam bath, fitness equipment, reiki treatments and massages alongside a pool and sauna. In summer, lots of activities are put on for children. 101 rooms | John Redmond Street | tel. 021 4 52 92 00 | www.maldronhotels.com | Moderate

METROPOLE

This centennial hotel with a slightly crumbling elegance lies on the northern bank of the river. Both pubs have singing in the evening, breakfast is taken with a view of the river. Nearby: a large leisure centre and several good restaurants. 98 rooms | MacCurtain Street | tel. 021 4 64 37 00 | www.gresham-hotels.com | Expensive

INFORMATION

TOURIST OFFICE

42 Grand Parade | tel. 021 4 25 51 00 | www.corkkerry.ie, www.cometocork.com

WHERE TO GO

BALTIMORE (133 D6) (🔊 C17)

Heading southwest from Cork for a good 60 miles leads through picturesque river valleys and undulating hills to the romantic coast. Starting from Cork you first hit Clonakilty (overnight at O'Donovan's Hotel | 26 rooms | tel. 023 8 33 32 50 | Pearse Street | www.odonovanshotel.com | Moderate), then Skibbereen before reaching Baltimore, the gateway to the islands of Sherkin and Clear. The small port town of Baltimore awakens in the spring, with the arrival of sailing and fishing visitors. During Fiddle Fair (www.fiddlefair.com) on the second weekend in May tradi-

There is a near-Mediterranean atmosphere about Bantry House and its surroundings

tional and modern music awaits. If you miss the foot-passenger ferry *(to Sherkin hourly | crossing 15 min | 10 euros return | www.sherkinferry.com; to Cape Clear two to three times a day | 45 min | 15 euros return | www.capeclearferry.com)*, you can stay overnight in Baltimore, e. g. in an imaginatively restored farm house *(Rolf's Country House | 14 rooms | Baltimore Hill | tel. 028 2 00 94 | www.rolfscountryhouse. eu | Budget)*. For over two decades, the best choice amongst Baltimore's restaurants has been *Chez Youen (The Quay | tel. 028/20 13 | Expensive)*, serving the finest Breton fish cuisine, e.g. scallops au gratin.

BANTRY (133 D5) *(𝄞 C17)*

In Bantry (57 mi west, pop 2800), ● *Bantry House* is worth a detour. The pretty castle was purchased in 1739 by the ancestors of the current owners. Over time, it was furnished with stylish wall

hangings, paintings and furniture. Italianate terraced gardens with fountains and statues surround the estate. There is a café and crafts shop. Two guest wings allow you to INSIDERTIP stay overnight in style – with the family at hand, and a round of croquet after breakfast. *Hotel 8 rooms | house and garden open to the public, March–Oct daily 10am–6pm | admission 10 euros | tel. 027 5 00 47 | www. bantryhouse.ie | Expensive*

BLARNEY CASTLE ★ ↯
(133 F4) *(𝄞 E16)*

5.5 miles west of Cork, the stronghold erected by Cormac McCarthy in 1446 dominates a park. The castle was restored to allow visitors to reach the famous *Blarney Stone* at 95 ft up, and after a fair bit of squiggling, to kiss it. Nearly everybody does that too, as the stone is said to lend the kisser the gift of the gab (*blarney* of course, meaning 'chatter, bla'...). Walking trails lead from the castle into the park, which includes a flower garden called *Rock Close* with rock formations considered to have a mythical significance. In summer, the Big House is open to visitors. *Park and castle daily 9am–7pm | admission 10 euros | www. blarneycastle.ie*

The pretty little village of *Blarney* is best known for the souvenirs sold from the *Woollen Mills* shop in a restored factory. Accommodation and restaurant are available at the *Blarney Park Hotel* with a large pool and gym *(76 rooms | Blarney | tel. 021 4 38 52 81 | Expensive)*.

CAPE CLEAR (132 C6) *(𝄞 C18)*

Lonely Ireland: fewer than 200 people live on this small island ('Oileán Chléire' in Irish) a good 60 miles southwest of Cork (ferry from Baltimore). *St Kieran's Stone* stands at the well, and there is a shrine for the island's patron saint of the same name. A steep path leads from the mooring up to the 12th-century ⚜ *St Kieran's Church*. To find further prehistoric monoliths, head for the eastern side of the island and *St Comillane*. The western coast boasts the ruined *O'Driscoll's Castle* dating back to the 14th century. *www.oilean-chleire.ie*

Mary Anne's pub to the left of the steep main street has already been lauded in the New York Times – and rightly so. When it's sunny, you can sit in the courtyard and enjoy fabulous fish and seafood. The old *castle* in an overgrown park on the sea is still inhabited by the descendants of the founders. They rent out rooms

Cobh Harbour: the little town is particularly pretty seen from the water

CASTLETOWNSHEND (127 D6) (*ጠ D17*)

The small settlement on Castle Haven Bay, 60 miles southwest of Cork, boasts an architectural gem: erected in the 17th century, the *Bow Hall* manor house has been converted into a guesthouse by Americans. Get a glimpse of village history at the *St Barrahane* church with its romantic ancient cemetery: Somerville, Coghill, Chavasse and Townshend – influential families that have been in this area for centuries.

in their quarrystone cottages next to the castle, as well as in its eastern and western wing (*Castletownshend Guesthouse | The Castle | 7 rooms | tel. 028 36100 | www.castle-townshend.com | Budget*).

COBH (134 A 5–6) (*ጠ F16*)

The pretty port town on an island in extensive Cork Harbour, some 14 miles southeast of Cork, is connected with the mainland by a bridge. Up to 1950, it was from Cobh – pronounced 'cove' – that ocean liners took Irish emigrants to America. Many houses still date back to the heyday of shipping in the 19th century. 〰 *St Colman's* Gothic cathedral dominates the colourful houses from its vantage point on a steep plateau; its famous *glockenspiel* (47 bells) attracts many visitors. A boat trip of the harbour opens up the beauty of the place. Find out more about Cobh's history at the *Heritage Centre (daily 10am–6pm | admission 7.10 euros | tel. 021 4 81 35 91 | www.cobhheritage.com)* in the old Victorian train station. Cobh was the last port of call of the ill-fated Titanic in 2012, commemorated in a Titanic Trail.

FOTA ISLAND (134 A5) (*መ F16*)

Heading east from Cork in the direction of Midleton, turn right and cross a bridge to reach Fota Island, harbouring the *Fota Estate* with its manor house. The expertly restored house is open to the public *(admission 6 euros)*. Behind the house, an INSIDER TIP *Arboretum* was laid out. The skilfully landscaped park features massive trees as well as rare plants, including some tropical rarities. *April–Oct daily 10am–5pm | www.fotahouse.com*

SHERKIN 〰 (133 D6) (*መ C18*)

The island a good 60 miles southwest of Cork is a great place for quiet walks with views of the Atlantic. Archaeologically minded visitors can discover prehistoric rocks at *Slievemore* on the western side of the island and descend into Early Christian caves. The *Silver Strand* beach is tempting for a dip in the sea. Also worth seeing is the ruined Franciscan monastery (1460). And if you're looking for seclusion, head for the northern shore. *Daily ferries from Baltimore*

SCHULL (132 C6) (*መ C 17*)

Pronounced, and sometimes spelt 'skull', the lively market town 68 miles west of Cork is a popular holiday village with *bed & breakfasts* and new holiday apartments, as well as the jetty for the Cape Clear ferry with a protected harbour. Right on the pier you can buy fish, fresh off the trawler and smoked. Shops and cafés line the main street. A recommended pit-stop is the *Courtyard (Main Street)*. Alongside craft shops and a pub (playing jazz and folk music), this former grain mill with courtyard also houses a delicatessen (selling mild Irish raw-milk cheese) and a ☺ café restaurant serving excellent natural foods. This is also where you can pick up the free *Visitors' Guide Schull* with information on the area.

DOG RACING

On nine state-run courses the gracious ● greyhounds hare after a fake rabbit, six dogs in each of the eight to ten races that are held each evening. Nobody dresses up: fashion takes a back seat here. Some of the many small betting shops are one-man shows, whose owners take bets standing on beer crates.

Visitors pay 10 euros to get in and place a bet (stakes of 5 euros) on the winner. All larger towns have racecourses, e.g. *Cork's Greyhound Stadium (Wed/Thu/ Sat 7pm | Curraheen Park, Curraheen Road (off the N 25), 3 mi southwest of Cork city centre (bus no. 8) | tel. 021 4 54 30 95 | www.igb.ie/cork).*

WEST CORK GARDEN TRAIL ●
(132 C5–137 D6) (*ØØ C–D17*)

Between Kinsale and Glengarriff, a number of gardens have come together under the heading *West Cork Garden Trail*. A Japanese Kasuga lantern several metres high marks the entrance to the *Lassanaroe Garden* in the small fishing village of Skibbereen to prepare visitors for its extraordinary collection of rare types of bamboo. In the same village Lord and Lady Puttnam open their *River House Garden* with a Japanese boat house, orchids and rare plants from the Himalayas. Not all gardens are open all year round, some only open their gates by previous appointment. Two weeks in June however, all gardens are open, staging special events. *www.westcorkgardentrail.com*

YOUGHAL ★ (134 B5) (*ØØ F16*)

The pretty town of Youghal (pop. 6000) is situated on the estuary of the Blackwater River, a good 30 miles east of Cork. The arch of a four-storey clock tower (1777) spans the main street. Climb up the steep steps to the ☆ INSIDER TIP city wall, with foundations dating back to the 13th century. From up here you get good views across the town with many 18th and 19th-century houses. A walk along the city wall passes several defensive towers, before arriving at *St Mary's Church*. Also dating from the 13th century, this stone-built church is well preserved. Said to have been founded as early as 450, the interior of the church is a treasure trove for those interested in Irish history! Below the church, the (private) *Myrtle Grove* was one of the residences of Sir Walter Raleigh (who is credited with bringing the potato to Ireland). If you have time, head for the harbour (Market Square) to visit the *Court House*, the elongated *Market House* as well as the *Water Gate*.

KILLARNEY

(132–133 C–D 4) (*ØØ C16*) **There's no doubt about it: the most beautiful thing about Killarney is the nature around it. Lying in a valley, the town is framed by three lakes: Lough Leane, Muckross Lake and Lough Guitane.**

Numerous rivers feed the waters amidst the near-evergreen vegetation. The backdrop is formed by several peaks, amongst them the *Macgillycuddy's Reeks* with Carrantouhill, at 3412 ft Ireland's highest mountain. The fabulously beautiful landscape, a great national park, as well as *Muckross House,* a classy manor house, have made Killarney (pop. 14,500) what it is today: a thoroughly commercialised tourist town.

Each year during the short summer season, holidaymakers flood into the town, creating logjams already outside the town's limits. At least cars are banned from Killarney's town centre in summer between 7pm and 8am. ● There is no escaping the *jaunting cars*, whose drivers shout out offers for sightseeing drives to destinations inside *Killarney National Park*.

SIGHTSEEING

GAP OF DUNLOE

Rocks, green mountains and lakes dominate the broad gorge running between the MacGillycuddy's Reeks to the west and Purple Mountain to the east at the exit of Killarney National Park. The starting point of a popular hike is the historic *Kate Kearney's Cottage (www.katekearneyscottage.com)* with pub and restaurant. From here a narrow road winds through a rough rocky near-alpine landscape. The horse-and-cart outfits take about an hour for the 5.5-

mile tour leading past three lakes (Black Lake, Cushnavalley Lake and Auger Lake); there are horse-riding options too.

MUCKROSS HOUSE ★

Built in 1843 by Scottish architect William Burn in the Victorian style for the Herbert family in an idyllic location on the shores of Muckross Lake, Muckross House is the country's most famous manor house. In 1964 it was made accessible to the public. Alongside rooms serving as a folk museum and to display old skills and crafts (weaving, pottery, blacksmithing), the rest of the castle-like mansion is kept in the style of around 1900 *(daily 9am–6pm | admission incl. guided tour 7 euros | 3 mi south on the N 71 | www.muckross-house.ie).* Access to Muckross House through the park is pretty all year round, but particularly spectacular in May when the rhododendrons are in bloom. The surrounding *Killarney National Park* (several entrances) offers fabulous hikes, to the ruined 15th-century monastery of *Muckross Abbey* for instance, to *Torc Waterfall* and the *Old Weir Bridge* (signposted). The area of the national park, spanning about 25,000 acres, was handed over to the state in 1932, together with Muckross House. Today, the park boasting Ireland's largest oak forest is under Unesco protection as a biosphere reserve. Several local operators (such as *www.southwestwalks ireland.com*) offer guided walks; details from the tourist information in Killarney and at *www.killarneynationalpark.ie.*

Discover the splendour of the Victorian era: Muckross House

ROSS CASTLE

Built in the 15th century, this impressive castle features two round towers and strong defensive walls. Guided tours let you see the antique oak furniture and tell the castle's interesting history. Pretty lakeside location. *March–Oct 9.30am–5.30pm | admission 6 euros | Ross Road, Bay of Ross, Lower Lake | 1.2 m southwest of Killarney*

FOOD & DRINK

CHAPTER FORTY

Walnut parquet and contemporary design set the scene for modern Irish cuisine. The exclusive menu changes frequently; imaginative delicious dishes. Book ahead! *Tue–Sat from 5pm onwards | 40 New Street | tel. 064 6 67 18 33 | Expensive*

GABY'S SEAFOOD

Being small didn't stop this fine fish restaurant from receiving the 'Irish Seafood Award'. The house speciality is lobster – which you can choose yourself from one of the tanks. *Mon–Sat | 27 High St. | tel. 064 6 63 25 19 | Expensive*

MAC'S

Opens for breakfast. Lunch sees a changing menu involving fish, chicken, pasta and grill dishes as well as 30 flavours of ice cream. *6 Main St. | tel. 064 6 63 52 13 | www.macsofmainstreet.com | Moderate*

INSIDER TIP MUCKROSS GARDEN RESTAURANT

Chicken with Clonakilty black pudding or *apple pie* with vanilla ice cream straight from the oven – everything they serve here tastes good. Add to that the idyllic location at the back of Muckross House: you can either sit in the rustic modern restaurant, the light-filled conservatory or – even better – on the terrace, furnished with teak chairs and tables. *Muckross House, Killarney National Park | tel. 064 6 67 01 44 | Moderate*

SCÉAL EILE

Good-value fare on a self-service basis. Head upstairs to the first floor for a good restaurant. *73 High Street | tel. 064 6 63 50 66 | Moderate*

SHOPPING

KILLARNEY BOOKSHOP

Travel literature, Irish novels, second-hand books, fairytales and myths. *32 Main Street | www.killarneybookshop.ie*

LEISURE & SPORTS

INSIDER TIP DONOGHUES' BOAT TOURS

Pat will take you in small boats (6–8 people) to Innisfallen Island *(1 hr | 7.50*

LOW BUDGET

▶ Simple restaurant with take-away in Killarney, serving excellent good-value dishes: at the *Genting* you'll find the whole range of Thai curries, as well as fish and crustaceans. *Innisfallen Shopping Mall, Main St. | tel. 064 3 70 00 | www.gentingthai.ie*

▶ Inexpensive accommodation in Killarney: *Neptune's Hostel* near the High Street offers dorms as well as en-suite doubles. *150 beds | Bishop's Lane, off New Street | tel. 064 6 63 52 55 | www.neptuneshostel.com*

The medieval ruined Ross Castle occupies a beautiful position on a green peninsula

euros), followed by a stop-off at the *Meeting of the Waters*, a pretty river landscape that inspired Thomas Moore to write his famous poem of the same name *(1.5–2 hrs / 10 euros). From Ross Castle | tel. 064 6 63 10 68 | www.killarneydaytour.com*

KILLARNEY RIDING STABLES
Alongside horses (hunters, ponies), the stables also offer accommodation in the farmhouse and trail riding over several days. *Ballydowney | 1.2 mi west of town on the N 72 | tel. 064 6 63 16 86 | www. killarney-reeks-trail.com*

KILLARNEY WATERCOACH
One-hour boat trip on Lough Leane between Innisfallen Island and Darby's Gardens. Departure point: *Ross Castle. Bus service by Destination Killarney, Scott's Gardens. East Ave. Road | departures every 90 min between 10.30am and 4.30pm | 10 euros, tickets also available from the tourist office*

ENTERTAINMENT

KILLARNEY GRAND
In the evenings, the hotel's own traditional pub is buzzing with Irish folk and, on Thursdays, traditional dance. International DJs spin their wares here too sometimes. *Main Street | tel. 064 6 63 11 59 | www.killarneygrand.com*

WHERE TO STAY

INSIDER TIP ▶ EARLS COURT HOUSE
Fine guesthouse decorated in 19th-century style on the edge of town towards Muckross. Romantics will love the interior: some of the rooms have a fireplace and four-poster bed. Opulent breakfast. *30 rooms | Woodlawn Junction Muckross Rd. | tel. 064 6 63 40 09 | www.killarney-earlscourt.ie | Moderate*

GLENA HOUSE
Pretty *bed & breakfast* with bistro-style restaurant, tea and coffee-making facilities in the room, car park. It's a five-minute walk

to the centre of town. *26 rooms | 23 Muck-ross Road | tel. 064 6 63 27 05 | Budget*

KILLARNEY PARK HOTEL
At this five-star country house, enjoy the coffee from silver pots with a view of the mountains and historic Killarney, *afternoon tea* at the open fire or treatments at the spa. *68 rooms | Town Centre, East Avenue Road | tel. 064 6 63 55 55 | www. killarneyparkhotel.ie | Expensive*

THE EUROPE HOTEL & RESORT ●
For lovers of design and nature: panoramic windows make the sea and the mountains become one with the spacious lobby; the gleaming chrome bar is reminiscent of Philippe Starck, the library a cave clad in black, with precious coffee-table books, and the Spa Centre with huge pool the most beautiful in the entire region. *187 rooms | Fossa, N 72 to Killorglin, 3 mi west of Killarney | tel. 064 6 67 13 40 | www.theeurope.com | Expensive*

INFORMATION

TOURIST INFORMATION OFFICE
Beech Road, off New Street | tel. 064 6 63 16 33 | www.killarney.ie

WHERE TO GO

BEARA PENINSULA
(132 B6–C5) (*ΩΩ B 17–C16*)
Jutting out into the sea between Bantry Bay and Kenmare, south of the Ring of Kerry, the harsh and wild Beara Peninsula awaits. The road snaking along the peninsula, the INSIDER TIP *Ring of Beara* is much less busy than the more popular routes around the Ring of Kerry and Dingle.
The excellent ● *Dzogchen Beara* meditation centre which follows the Tibetan-Buddhist tradition above the dramatic coastal cliffs is open to interested visitors.

There are daily (9–9.45am) free guided meditations, also weekend retreats (190 euros incl. food) and annual workshops with the spiritual leader Sogyal Rinpoche, author of the bestselling The Tibetan Book of Living and Dying. Accommodation is available at the hostel or in cottages *(Garranes, Allihies | tel. 027 73 00 32 | www.dzogchenbeara.org | Budget)*.
On the southwest point of the peninsula, the INSIDER TIP *SA Dursey Cable Car (Windy Point House | Allihies | Mon–Sat 9–10.30am, 2.30–4.30pm, 7–7.30pm, Sun 9–10am, 1–2pm, 7–7.30pm | crossing 4 euros (return)* takes visitors onto Dursey Island, a trip of 374 m that might feel long to some. The island, covering 4 by 1 miles, has only a handful of inhabitants, no pub, guesthouse or restaurant. A 7-mile hiking trail, allowing you to spot many seabirds, leads past the lighthouse and around the island. *www.bearatourism.com*

INSIDER TIP BLASKET ISLANDS
(132 A3) (*ΩΩ A15*)
Up until 1953 these islands were inhabited by an Irish-speaking community that published over a dozen books. Some of them are available from the *Blasket Centre* in *Dunquin* (admission 3.70 euros) on the mainland. In the house of Peig Sayers – whose classic memoir was the bane of many an Irish schooling – tea is served today. Boat tours around the Blasket Islands with the chance to see whales, dolphins and seals *(3 hours | daily 1pm | 30 euros)* and ferry service to the Blasket Islands *(daily 10am–5pm hourly | crossing time 15 min | 25 euros return)* from Dunquin through *Eco Marine Adventure Tour (tel. 087 2 31 61 31 | www.blasket islands.ie). 55 mi west of Killarney*

DINGLE (132 B3) (*ΩΩ B15*)
The capital of the peninsula of the same name to the west (44 mi) is a lively

market town (pop. 1500) with a pretty natural harbour. Alongside B&Bs and hostels, a stylish accommodation option is *Benner's Hotel*, a townhouse with comfortable rooms and a popular pub *(52 rooms | Main St. | tel. 066 9 15 16 38 | www.dinglebenners.com | Expensive)*. Covering some 93 miles, the *Dingle Way* hiking trail (see Trips & Tours, page 96) leads past sandy beaches and mountain ranges. The narrow windy coastal road leading around the peninsula leads to several archaeological sites.

GLENGARRIFF (132 C5) (*𝄞 C17*)

Palm trees and fuchsia hedges adorn the village (pop. 800) on the estuary where the Glengarriff River flows into Bantry Bay; plenty of tourists visit during the summer months. The terrace café of the Victorian *Eccles Hotel (66 rooms | Glengarriff Harbour | tel. 027 6 30 03 | www.eccleshotel.com | Moderate)* affords a view of Glengarriff Bay. Right opposite the hotel, every 20 minutes the Harbour Queen *(March–Oct | 12 euros)* leaves for Garinish Island *(www.garnishisland.com)*. Covering 37 acres, the island is famous for its Mediterranean garden architecture with Greek temples, tree ferns reaching 2 metres and rare subtropical trees.

RING OF KERRY ★
(132 B–C 3–5) (*𝄞 B–C 15–16*)

The famous Ring of Kerry is a unique coastal and panoramic road leading for some 125 miles around the Iveragh Peninsula. The road is so narrow that buses are only allowed to use it driving in one direction. In order to properly enjoy the sublime landscape, try and schedule at least two days for a visit. Fabulous views across ☀ *Dingle Bay* open up on the section between Glenbeigh and Cahersiveen. The fishing village of Glenbeigh, 7.5 miles west of Killorglin, is the starting point

Spectacular views of the Dingle Peninsula's steep coastline

for trekking and hiking routes across the Macgillycuddy's Reeks and around Caragh Lake. A lovely hiking tour leads from Seefin in a semicircle to Drung Hill across a fantastic landscape of lakes and hills with panoramic sea views. Beach life can be enjoyed at the long safe Rossbeigh Beach. Overnight accommodation is available at the *Olde Glenbeigh Hotel (12 rooms | tel. 066 9 76 83 33 | www.glenbeighhotel.com | Moderate)*.

From Portmagee, a bridge leads to *Valentia Island*, a place of huge fuchsias, rhododendrons and brambles, with wide plains in between. *Knightstown*, the island's largest town and starting point for fishing and diving tours, has a fairly sleepy vibe. A paradise for anglers on the mainland is *Waterville*, which lies as in a lagoon between the sea and a lake. Numerous hiking trails lead around *Lough Currane* and into the mountains beyond. At the southern start of the Ring of Kerry, Kenmare Bay, the pretty town of *Kenmare* (pop. 2500) features some limestone houses with lavish decoration. Fish restaurants and craft shops line the few streets. With the *Caha Mountains* as a backdrop, the opulent ● *Kenmare Park Hotel* country house boasts gardens reaching down to Kenmare Bay. The Victorian hotel's top spa features zen gardens, a pool and ayurvedic treatments. *46 rooms | Kenmare Bay | tel. 064 6 64 12 00 | www.parkkenmare.com | Expensive*

`INSIDER TIP` Visitors travelling by car and wanting to follow the Ring of Kerry by the *Cliffs of Moher* can save the detour via Limerick with the car ferry from Tarbert to Killimer *(7am–9pm half-hourly to hourly | crossing time 20 minutes | 18 euros per car incl. passengers | www.shannonferries. com)*. The new Limerick road tunnel however has more or less levelled the times.

SKELLIG MICHAEL ★
(132 A5) (*ŵ A16*)
One of the most beautiful medieval monasteries in Ireland lies on this difficult-to-access island jutting out of the sea 7.5 miles off the coast: ☼ Skellig Michael (also called *Great Skellig*). The monastic settlement founded there in the 7th century belongs to Unesco World Heritage and was inhabited for 600 years. 670 steps (without a rail) lead up to it, offering sheer breathtaking views. A little closer to the coast, the neighbouring island of *Little Skellig* shelters the world's second-largest gannet colony. There are boat services between the mainland and Skellig Michael (the crossing is dependent on the weather!). The boat circles Little Skellig on the return journey, but is not allowed land there. Departure from Portmagee and Knightstown (30–50 euros). *Skellig Experience Centre, Island Bridge, Valentia Island | May–Sept 10am–5pm, July/Aug to 7pm | admission 5 euros, round trip 27.50 euros | tel. 066 9 47 63 06 | www.skelligexperience.com*

KINSALE

(133 F5) (*ŵ E17*) ★ **This is a picture-postcard kind of a place: Kinsale is an all-round pretty port (pop. 4000) with colourful rows of houses along narrow winding streets, a flower-bedecked seafront promenade and sailing yachts in the harbour.**

In the sports and society calendar, the sailing regatta in August is the top event in the region. The rest of the time, Kinsale attracts visitors to its numerous pubs and excellent if pricey restaurants. The town prides itself on being Ireland's culinary capital.

SIGHTSEEING

CHARLES FORT ☼
A pleasant one-hour walk of almost two miles along the bay on the eastern side of the harbour through Scilly and Summercove leads to the British *fort*. The imposing star-shaped fortification from the year 1677 is well preserved. *James Fort* (1602) is reached across a bridge. *June–Sept daily 9am–6pm, April, May, Oct Sat–Mon 11am–5pm | admission 4 euros | Summercove*

KINSALE MUSEUM
In the former courthouse (1706), displays bring to life the town's history from megalithic settlement to the Battle of Kinsale

fought by the British against the Spanish. *June–Oct Wed–Sat 10am–5pm, Sun 2–5pm, Nov–May Wed–Sat 11am–2pm, Sun 2–5pm | admission 2.50 euros | Old Court House Market Square*

ST MULTOSE

This church built in the 12th century by the Normans is the town's oldest building. The cemetery shelters some of the 1198 victims of the Lusitania disaster. The torpedoing of a passenger liner by a German U-boat in 1915 triggered America's entry into the First World War. *Church Street*

FOOD & DRINK

THE BULMAN

Contemporary Irish cuisine (local fish specialities and crustaceans) with harbour views. The ground floor is occupied by a 200-year-old pub, in the summer life moves outside. *Summercove | tel. 021 4772131 | www.thebulman.com | Moderate*

INSIDER TIP ▶ FISHY FISHY CAFÉ

Some say this is Ireland's best fish restaurant. What is true that the best seafood of the south is served up here, prawns with *smoked salmon sandwiches* and fresh brown sodabread. Try your own hand at cooking the recipes once back home with the Irish Seafood Cookery Book by owner Martin Shanahan available from the restaurant. *Pier Road (on the harbour) | tel. 021 4700415 | www.fishyfishy.ie | Moderate*

PIER ONE

Views across the harbour, daily changing menu and fresh fish every day. *At the Trident Hotel, World's End | tel. 021 4779300 | www.tridenthotel.com | Moderate*

SHOPPING

BOLAND

Whether Aran sweaters, pottery or jewellery: discover a large range of Irish

Nothing fishy here: the Fishy Fishy Café serves excellent seafood

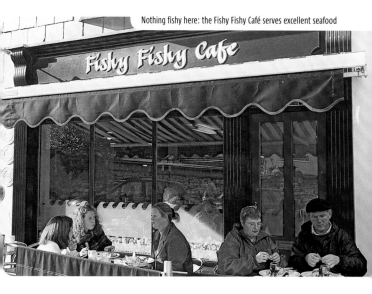

crafts and souvenirs. *1 Pearse Street | www.bolandkinsale.com*

LEISURE & SPORTS

KINSALE HARBOUR CRUISES
Board the *Spirit of Kinsale* for a trip around the harbour, past the fort and the Old Town. *Daily departures from the quay between Actons Hotel (300 m) and the marina | timetable at tourist office | 12.50 euros | www.kinsaleharbourcruises.com*

place for young and old. Delicious dishes include *seafood chowder and bacon & cabbage. Scilly | tel. 021 4 77 24 36 | www. thespaniard.ie*

WHERE TO STAY

ACTONS HOTEL
Comfortable hotel on the harbour, with spa, pool and gym. Golf and fishing trips can be arranged. *73 rooms | Pier Road | tel. 021 4 77 99 00 | www.actons*

The evening sun turns the stone walls of King John's Castle on the River Shannon golden

OUTDOOR EDUCATION CENTRE
Sailing, windsurfing, canoe tours, mountaineering, freeclimbing, discovering nature and much more, classes for beginners and advanced levels. *St John's Hill | tel. 021 4 77 31 21 | www.kinsaleoutdoors.com*

ENTERTAINMENT

THE SPANIARD
Everything is just so in this self-styled *'olde worlde inn of character and charm'.* Located above the harbour, this cosily furnished pub restaurant is a meeting

hotelkinsale.com | Moderate

OLD BANK HOUSE
This Georgian townhouse is the most stylish amongst Kinsale's luxury hotels. The cosy rooms are furnished with antiques, paintings and plush upholstery, and have a very personal touch. *17 rooms | 11 Pearse Street | tel. 021 4 77 40 75 | www. oldbankhousekinsale.com | Expensive*

TIERNEY'S GUESTHOUSE
Light-filled friendly rooms in a pretty Georgian townhouse. The excellent *Irish*

breakfast is served in the conservatory. *10 rooms | 70 Main Street | tel. 021 4 77 22 05 | www.tierneys-kinsale.com | Moderate*

TRIDENT

Lavishly renovated mid-range hotel with a view of fishing trawlers and sailing boats from every room. *75 rooms | World's End | tel. 021 4 77 93 00 | www.tridenthotel.com | Moderate*

INFORMATION

TOURIST OFFICE

Pier Road | tel. 021 4 77 22 34 | www.kinsale.ie

LIMERICK

MAP INSIDE THE BACK COVER (133 F1) *(E14)* **Since millions of euros were spent in recuperating and restoring public buildings, and the opening of new chic hotels, restaurants and shops, Ireland's third-largest city (pop. 91,000) exudes a new self-confidence.**
Limerick also happens to be the country's oldest settlement. The Normans erected city walls and castles and constructed a bridge across the Shannon. In the 18th century, Limerick was given its current aspect: with broad streets and imposing townhouses in the Georgian style.
A few miles north of the city, Shannon Airport is handy for visitors wanting to travel the southwest of Ireland, as well as Galway and the Shannon region.

WHERE TO START?
Patrick Street: stroll from here to King John's Castle via a tributary of the River Shannon. If arriving by hire car, the best place to park is at Arthur's Quay in front of the tourist office on the River Shannon. Trains arrive at Colbert Station, a few minutes on foot outside the city centre.

SIGHTSEEING

HUNT MUSEUM

Private art collection including numerous archaeological finds testifying to the Celtic sense of ornamentation and decoration, also works by Leonardo da Vinci, Auguste Renoir and W B Yeats, housed in the stylish *Old Customs House*. There's a good restaurant here too. *Mon–Sat 10am–5pm, Sun 2–5pm | admission 8 euros | www.huntmuseum.com | Rutland Street*

JIM KEMMY MUNICIPAL MUSEUM (LIMERICK CITY MUSEUM)

Located next to the main entrance to King John's Castle, the city museum presents Limerick's history from the Bronze Age and the Viking invasion to the present day. *Tue–Sat 10am–1pm, 2.15–5pm | free admission | Castle Lane, off Nicholas Street | www.limerick.ie/citymuseum*

KING JOHN'S CASTLE

Built in the early 13th century by the Normans on the banks of the river Shannon, the castle used to have four round towers, one of which was subsequently converted into the bastion. Today, steps replace the former drawbridge. The skilfully restored castle also houses the city museum. *March–Oct daily 9.30am–5pm, Nov–Feb 10am–4pm | admission 9.45 euros | Castle Parade, King's Island, off Nicholas Street*

ST MARY'S CATHEDRAL

Visit the Protestant church built in 1172 by Donald Mor O'Brian for its Gothic leaded glass and fine choir stalls. *In summer Mon–Sat 9am–5pm, in winter 9am–1pm | Bridge Street | suggested donation 2 euros | www.cathedral.limerick.anglican.org*

INSIDER TIP **WALKING TOURS**

Guided walks to a dozen sights are offered by the *St Mary's Action Centre. Daily 11am and 2.30pm | 44 Nicholas Street | tel. 061 41 16 56 | 10 euros*

FOOD & DRINK

FREDDY'S BISTRO

Italian and Irish cuisine in a stylish building of natural stone; vegetarians are well catered for as well. Recommended: the *Irish Guinness stew. Tue–Sun from 6pm | Theatre Lane, off Lower Glentworth Street | tel. 061 418749 | www.freddys bistro.com | Expensive*

MARKET SQUARE

Fine Irish fare served at the fireplace of a vaulted cellar. *Tue–Sat | 74 O'Connell Street | tel. 061 31 63 11 | Expensive*

MORTELLS DELICATESSEN & SEAFOOD

Seafood specialities such as mussels, oysters or langoustines, plus *carvery lunch. Daily 8.30am–6pm | 49 Roches Street | tel. 061 41 54 57 | Moderate*

SHOPPING

IRISH HANDCRAFTS

Family-run operation specialising in tweed, fine linen and unusual woven textiles. *26 Patrick Street | www.irish-handcrafts.com*

ENTERTAINMENT

DOLAN'S PUB & THE WAREHOUSE

Traditional music at the pub, Sun from 6pm, Tue with dancing. If you are looking for other types of concerts and a nightclub, head for the INSIDER TIP Warehouse right next door. *Start usually 10pm | tickets 5–20 euros | 3/4 Dock Road | tel. 061 31 44 83 | www.dolanspub.com*

WHERE TO STAY

THE GEORGE

This city-centre boutique hotel embodies Limerick's new image: chic, cosmopolitan, modern. Some of the rooms have an open fire. Guests meet for a pint in George's Bar. *124 rooms | O'Connell Street | tel. 061 46 04 00 | www.the-georgeboutiquehotel.com | Moderate*

KILMURRY LODGE

Rustic country house atmosphere with a touch of Laura Ashley: this quiet genteel hotel is situated a bit outside the city, surrounded by extensive green spaces and close to the university. *100 rooms | Dublin Road, N 7, Castletroy | tel. 061 33 11 33 | www.kilmurrylodge.com | Moderate*

RAILWAY HOTEL

Opposite the train and bus station. Basic en-suite rooms, parking behind the house. *30 rooms | Parnell Street | tel. 061 41 36 53 | www.railwayhotel.ie | Budget*

INFORMATION

TOURIST OFFICE

Arthur's Quay | tel. 061 31 75 22 | www.limerick.ie

WHERE TO GO

ADARE (133 E1) (*Ω E14*)

'Ireland's prettiest village', Adare (pop. 700), some 11 miles southwest of Limerick enchants with thatched cottages and picturesque peasant gardens. *Adare*

Manor, an estate built in the Gothic style, boasts 75 chimneys and countless leaded windows. The *Adare Heritage Centre (daily 9am–6pm | Main St. | admission 5 euros | www.adareheritagecentre.ie)* sells crafts too.

BUNRATTY CASTLE ● (133 E1) (*ﾉﾉ E13*)

The famous restored castle some 10 miles northwest (on the N 18 in the direction of Ennis) has precious antique furniture. Twice a day *(5.30pm and 9pm)*, medieval banquets with musical accompaniment are put on. Extending immediately behind the castle, *Bunratty Folk Park* is a replica of an Irish 19th-century village. *Daily 9am–5.30pm (castle to 4pm) | admission 15.75 euros (castle and park)*

CRAGGAUNOWEN (129 D6) (*ﾉﾉ E13*)

Some 19 miles northwest of the city, it is worth visiting the open-air museum with a Bronze Age settlement on an artificial island (*crannog*), a 5th-century ringfort with farmstead and the boat used by explorer Tim Severin for his 1976 sailing from Ireland to Greenland, in order to prove that the Celts could have discovered America before Columbus did. The imposing *Craggaunowen Castle* rises up on a crag above the lake. *May–Sept daily 10am–5pm | admission 9 euros | www. craggaunowen.org*

LOUGH GUR (133 F2) (*ﾉﾉ E14*)

The borders of this small lake, some 12 miles south of Limerick, are one of the most important archaeological sites in the country. Thousands of objects from the Stone Age excavated here are now exhibited at the *Stone Age Centre*. There are also models of burial chambers and stone circles, as well as tools and prehistoric pottery. *May–Sept daily 10.30am–5pm | admission 5 euros | www.loughgur.com*

Typical for Adare village: thatched cottages

THE WEST COAST

The west of Ireland is something special: the basalt and granite Cliffs of Moher dropping down into the ocean along a stretch of 5 miles. And the Burren, a rocky plateau with caves and subterranean corridors that many compare to a lunar landscape, fascinates visitors with its unique rare plants as well as testimonies to Early Christian times.

On the Aran Islands, a lonely cliff fort exudes a mythical atmosphere, while Connemara stands for charmingly dramatic coastal and mountainous landscapes. In Galway, the region also offers a typically Irish metropolis: a vibrant harbour city, said by the Irish to have Mediterranean flair. What you will certainly discover there is an exciting arts scene and much joie de vivre.

GALWAY

(128 C4) (*D11*) Summer in Galway (pop. 72,000) is a time of festivities and events, whether the Galway Races in July or the Arts Festival, where the entire city becomes a mecca for the arts. Come for the Galway Oyster Festival and help the locals wolf down the best oysters in Ireland with rivers of Guinness. Colourful old houses in the compact Old Town, friendly people, some of them even speaking Irish amongst themselves: Galway embodies Ireland in the nicest way, including the ability to bring together tradition and the 21st century. People from all over the world throng the cafés on Eyre Square, so alongside traditional *singing pubs* and

Photo: Inishmore: the biggest of the Aran Islands

Lunar landscapes and lakes teeming with fish: discover unspoilt nature while biking, hiking and relaxing

basic *bed & breakfasts* there is an increasing selection of hip hotels and restaurants. Even the inevitable rain is said to be more fun in Galway than elsewhere.

SIGHTSEEING

GALWAY CITY MUSEUM

A new glass-fronted building shows over 1000 exhibits telling the story of the city over thousands of years. Most were gifted by citizens of Galway. Excellent view of the city and harbour from the 🌿 terrace.

Mon 2–5pm, Tue–Sat 10am–5pm | free admission | Spanish Parade at Spanish Arch | www.galwaycitymuseum.ie

KIRWAN'S LANE

The most beautiful medieval alley in Galway has been sensitively restored and is lined by shops, residential housing and restaurants. *Off Quay Street*

LYNCH'S MEMORIAL WINDOW

In 1493, Mayor James Lynch declared his son guilty of having killed a Span-

Patience...: their wives are probably still browsing in the boutique

iard out of jealousy. As nobody could be found who wanted to execute the son, the father took matters into his own hands – literally. Since this day, it is said that the vocabulary of the people of Galway, and later everybody else, acquired the expression 'lynching'. A window arch with memorial plaque in the wall of St Nicholas Church is a reminder of the event. *Market Street*

ST NICHOLAS CHURCH
The country's largest medieval church dates back to the year 1320. According to legend, Columbus is said to have prayed here with his men before setting sail again for America. *Market Street | www. stnicholas.ie*

FOOD & DRINK

DRUID LANE
Cottage feeling at the open fireplace: your host Camilla Cutlar serves up wine and tapas on the ground floor of a medieval red-washed sandstone house, while the first floor is given over to seafood, burgers and pasta. *9 Quay Street | tel. 091 56 30 15 | www.druidlanerestaurant. com | Moderate*

INSIDER TIP KC BLAKE
Stylish restaurant in a medieval stone building. The fare here is a blend of down-to-earth and innovative Irish cooking with fish, seafood, steaks and lamb ragouts. *10 Quay Street | tel. 091 56 18 26 | Moderate*

KIRWAN'S
Creative cuisine in the new Irish style, way beyond cabbage & potatoes, in a medieval alley. *Kirwan's Lane, off Quay Street | tel. 091 56 82 66 | Expensive*

MCDONAGH'S SEAFOOD HOUSE
Even the New York Times is full of praise: they have been serving up fish and seafood – fresh off the boat and prepared in delicious ways, in an imposing *seafood platter, for example* – since 1902. For a cheaper option, choose the attached *fish & chips bar. 22 Quay Street | tel. 091 56 50 01 | www.mcdonaghs.net | Moderate*

SHOPPING

JUDY GREENE
(DESIGN CONCOURSE IRELAND)
Irish crafts and design: glassware, jewellery, ceramics, china, small items of home furniture and fabrics. *Kirwan's Lane*

TWICE AS NICE

Irish linen and hand-made lace (in the shape of tableware and bedlinen as well as clothing) are for sale in this colourful Old Town house. Also soaps made to old recipes, jewellery and antiques. *5 Quay Street | www.twiceasniceireland.com*

LEISURE & SPORTS

CLONBOO RIDING SCHOOL

Riding school for beginners and advanced riders. *Clonboo Cross, Headford Road, Corrundulla (N 84) | tel. 091 79 13 62*

ENTERTAINMENT

DRUID THEATRE

Small theatre in a former granary, also lunch-time performances. *Chapel Lane off Quay Street | tel. 091 56 86 60 | www.druidtheatre.com*

RÓISÍN DUBH

Near-legendary pub of the Irish rock'n'-roll scene, whose past greats pop up here again and again. Always live concerts, amongst them blues and folk too. *8 Upper Dominick Street | tel. 091 58 65 40 | www.roisindubh.net*

THE QUAYS

Pub with several bar areas. Cosy interior with maritime touch, leaded glass and Gothic arches. The *Old Bar* on the ground floor, playing traditional music, is a meeting place for students, while upstairs is given over to Dixie, rock and other styles. *Quay Street | tel. 091 56 83 47*

WHERE TO STAY

ARDILAUN HOUSE

Town palace dating back to 1840 and converted into a first-class hotel with pool and spa, tennis, squash, as well as pitch & putt. *125 rooms | Taylors Hill | tel. 091 52 14 33 | www.theardilaunhotel.ie | Moderate*

BARNACLE'S QUAY STREET HOUSE

From the pubs and shops of the pedestrian zone it's only a few steps to the double rooms or dorms with 6–12 (bunk) beds. Young travellers from all over the world appreciate the hostel's vibrant multicultural atmosphere. *112 beds | 10 Quay Street | tel. 091 56 86 44 | www.barnacles.ie | Budget*

PARK HOUSE

Luxury in a restored historic house with generously sized rooms in strong colours. For the past 25 years the restaurant has defended its position as one of the best in town. *84 rooms | Forster Street, near Eyre Square | tel. 091 56 49 24 | www.parkhousehotel.ie | Expensive*

MARCO POLO HIGHLIGHTS

⭐ **Aran Islands**
Three old-fashioned islands with Ireland's most beautiful ring fort right on the cliff edge → p. 74

⭐ **Burren**
Bare landscape with plants from three climate zones, exciting caves and subterranean rivers → p. 74

⭐ **Cliffs of Moher**
Here, Ireland's coast pulls out all the stops: the rocky walls jut up from the sea into the sky for up to 650 ft → p. 75

⭐ **Connemara**
Beaches on a fantastic coast, waterfalls – an undiluted nature experience for hikers → p. 75

SLEEPZONE HOSTEL

In the city centre: modern kitchen, terrace, laundrette, 24-hour access. Single rooms, double rooms and dorms (6–8 beds). *197 beds | Bothar na mBan (opposite Dyke Road) | tel. 091 56 69 99 | www.sleepzone.ie | Budget*

INSIDER TIP ▶ THE G HOTEL

Candy colours, a spot of Baroque fused with a touch of minimalism: this new luxury hotel likes to play with contrasts. Three interlocking lounges, a fabulous Asian-style spa across two floors with bamboo garden on the roof. *101 rooms | Wellpark (Dublin Road, R 338) | tel. 091 8 65 20 04 | www.theghotel.ie | Expensive*

THE WESTERN

Georgian guesthouse with large comfortable rooms and a popular pub. *40 rooms | Prospect Hill, near Eyre Square | tel. 091 56 28 34 | www.thewestern.ie | Moderate*

INFORMATION

TOURIST OFFICE

Forster Street, near Eyre Square | tel. 091 53 77 00 | www.galway.net and www.galwaytourist.com

WHERE TO GO

ARAN ISLANDS ★
(128 B4–5) (*ᗠ C12*)

Of the three Aran Islands – Inisheer, Inishmaan and Inishmore – lying opposite Galway Bay, the latter is the largest, covering some 18 sq miles. The bare Aran Islands (pop 1500) are known all over the country for their Celtic customs and as a stronghold of the Irish language. At least on the two smaller ones, time seems to have stood still. Inishmore boasts ● *Dun Aengus,* the most important and most beautiful stone fort in Ireland, in a fantastically dramatic position on the edge of sheer cliffs. Some visitors go down on their bellies to inch forward right to the edge of the abyss: over 300 ft below, the Atlantic is battering against the rocks. The islands are crisscrossed by skilfully layered stone walls that keep in the heat and protect from the wind. The famous Aran sweaters are for sale everywhere – and here is a good place to get them, but look for hand-knitted jumpers if you want the real deal. Guesthouses offer *bed & (full Irish) breakfast,* in the evening, life repairs to the pubs. *Daily ferry services from various ports, e. g. Doolin (www.doolinferries.com) and from Rossaveal (www.aranislandferries.com), 1 hr west of Galway; there are also flights with Aer Arann from the regional airport in Inverin (tel. 091 59 30 34 | www.aerarannislands.ie)*

A good place to stay is the *Ostan Arann (Aran Islands Hotel),* 400 m from the pier at Inishmore *(22 rooms | tel. 099 6 11 04 | www.aranislandshotel.com | Moderate),* a house clad in stone, with a restaurant and bar. ❧ INSIDER TIP ▶ Five balcony rooms have views of the bay and harbour.

BURREN ★ (128 C5) (*ᗠ D12*)

Stretching out across the northwest of County Clare, the *Burren,* an area of some 60 sq miles of bare limestone, appears like a lunar landscape. However, this is Ireland's Butterfly Central, and arctic and alpine plants grow next to each other; in summer even orchids flower here *(www.burrenbeo.ie).*

Right in the heart of the Burren, ● *Aillwee Cave* is an underground labyrinth of caves and rivers with numerous stalactites *(3 mi south of Ballyvaughan | daily 10am–6pm | www.aillweecave.ie | admission 17 euros).* Next to the cave, the *Burren Birds of Prey Centre* breeds and rears falcons, eagles, owls and other birds of prey.

A reminder of Ireland's early history,

when the Burren was still inhabited, are *ring forts* (circular walls of stone or soil) and *dolmens* (large stone 'tables') such as the *Poulnabrone Dolmen*. In the village of Kilfenora, the *Burren Centre* offers a permanent exhibition and an audiovisual presentation. A good option for accommodation is the hostel *Sleepzone – The Burren (124 beds | Kincora Road, Lisdoonvarna | tel. 065 7 07 40 36 | www. sleepzone.ie | Budget)*.

Yoga classes can be booked at the proactive ● *Burren Yoga Centre (Lig do Scith,*

the excellent *Atlantic Edge* exhibition. In good weather, climb ⚡ *O'Brien's Tower (admission 2 euros)* for views all the way to the Aran Islands. When there's a swell, look out for the huge surfing wave Aileens. *Nov–Feb 9am–5pm, March/April/ Sept to 6pm, May/June to 7pm, July–Aug 9am–9.30pm | admission 6 euros | www. cliffsofmoher.ie*

The Cliffs of Moher provide a habitat for huge colonies of birds. A one-hour INSIDER TIP ▶ boat tour with Arran Ferries allows you to view the cliffs from the wa-

Steep, steeper, Cliffs of Moher: jutting near-vertical out of the Atlantic

Normangrove, Cappaghmore near Kinvara, tel. 091/63 76 80 | www.burrenyoga. com). Yoga teachers from abroad often come here to teach.

CLIFFS OF MOHER ★ (128 B5) (⋈ C13)

Stretching over 5 miles, the Unescolisted Cliffs of Moher reach heights of up to 700 ft. There are many sections where they jut near-vertically out of the Atlantic. The *visitor centre* presents

ter, together with their abundant seabird life *(from Doolin harbour | April–Oct | 15 euros | tel. 065 7 07 59 49 | www.cliffs-of-moher-cruises.com)*.

CONNEMARA ★
(128 B 2–3) (⋈ C10–11)

Founded in 1812, the town of *Clifden* (pop. 1500) is the starting point for a biking tour of some 93 miles across the coastal route through Connemara, truly beautiful in parts, and for a visit to the mountain range of *The Twelve Pins* to the east. The barren landscape has a charm all of its own; low stone walls crisscross the fields, and the coastline itself is lined by beautifully white sandy beaches. Old country traditions live on in Connemara, and Irish is still spoken here too.

On the N59, between Recess and Letterfrack, you will find *Kylemore Abbey & Gardens*. Today, the beautiful 19th-

shows how the popular Irish folk music instrument is born. *Roundstone Musical Instruments | The Monastery | in summer daily, in winter Mon–Sat 9am–7pm | www.bodhran.com*

WESTPORT

(128 B1) (*ℳ C10*) **The drive through Gaelic Connemara leads to Westport**

The Twelve Pins mountain range crowns the rugged landscape of Connemara

century neo-Gothic fairytale castle is run as a girls' boarding school by a Benedictine order. Four rooms of the abbey, surrounded by green hills and lakes, as well as the Gothic church and the gardens are open to the public *(March–Oct 9am–6pm, Nov–Feb 10am–4pm | admission 12 euros | www.kylemoreabbey.com)*.

In an old Franciscan monastery in *Roundstone*, Malachy Kearns, the only Irishman who still makes INSIDER TIP bodhrán drums in the traditional way by hand,

on Clew Bay, a bay sprinkled with numerous small islands. The small town (pop. 3500), a Georgian gem, snuggles around an octagonal square and is divided by the channelled narrow Carrowbeg River. Founded in the 18th century, the town owed its prosperity to the trade in yarns and fabrics, and its port. In the 19th century, it lost out to the English textile industry and the building of a railway line from Dublin. Today, tourism is blossoming again.

SIGHTSEEING

OLD HARBOUR
Warehouses and quay infrastructure from Westport's founding days reflect the town's former economic heyday. *The Quay*

GEORGIAN RESIDENCES
Houses from the 18th and 19th centuries with well-preserved frontages line the main street, *The Mall*. The prettiest, with an impressive entrance portal, stands at the neo-Romanesque *St Mary's church*, which is also worth seeing.

OCTAGON
The main square has a fascinating geometrical structure, consisting of eight sides of equal length, of which three are divided by an intersecting street. The Doric column at its centre stands on an octagonal granite base and is topped by a young St Patrick.

WESTPORT HOUSE
Erected in 1731, the early Georgian manor house occupies a beautiful position with a view of Clew Bay. The bedrooms and dining rooms feature precious mahogany objects and Chinese tapestries from the 18th century, alongside glass objects and woodcarvings in Art Nouveau style. You'll find souvenirs for sale, as well as art and antiquities. Access from *The Quay*. *June–Aug daily 10am–6pm, May Sat/Sun 11am–5pm| admission 12.50 euros | www.westporthouse.ie*

FOOD & DRINK

ASGARD TAVERN & RESTAURANT
Long-established family concern in a pretty, whitewashed country house at the harbour. The cooking has won several awards for its hearty Irish specialities (lamb, salmon, farmhouse cheese) and fish dishes. Pub grub *(fish, chips and pies)* can be ordered from the attached pub. *The Quay | tel. 098 2 53 19 | Moderate*

CRONIN'S SHEEBEEN
The thatched restaurant and pub on Clew Bay exert a magic draw on lovers of fancy fish dishes (such as *seafood chowder* or fresh Clew Bay lobster). In the pub, guests meet for a Guinness and bar food snacks. *Rosberg | tel. 098 2 65 28 | Expensive*

INSIDER TIP ▶ QUAY COTTAGE
A nautical and rustic atmosphere pervades this restaurant in a historic cottage on Westport's harbour – a popular place to enjoy oysters and fish dishes. *The Quay, at the entrance to Westport House | tel. 098 2 64 12 | www.quaycottage.com | Moderate*

LOW BUDGET

▶ No charge: the very well-preserved 15th-century town palace of *Lynch's Castle* may be visited for free. *Galway | Shop Street*

▶ In a stone-built house the *Clew Bay* Heritage Centre in Westport presents objects, documents and photos about the history of Clew Bay. *April/May/Oct Mon–Fri 10am–2pm, June–Sept 10am–3pm, July/Aug also Sun 3–5pm | admission 3 euros | The Quay*

▶ The *Old Mill Holiday Hostel*, a pretty 18th-century quarrystone building in the heart of Westport, also offers good-value double rooms. *52 beds | Barrack Yard, James Street | tel. 098 2 70 45 | www.oldmillhostel.com*

ENTERTAINMENT

INSIDER TIP ▶ **MATT MOLLOY'S**

There's traditional music on a daily basis in the pub owned by Matt Molloy, who plays the flute with the famous Irish folk band The Chieftains. *Bridge Street | www.mattmolloy.com*

WHERE TO STAY

ARDMORE COUNTRY HOUSE

Small, well-run hotel with a cosy atmosphere. The restaurant affords pretty views of the hills and Clew Bay. *13 rooms | The Quay | tel. 098 25 99 | www.ardmorecountryhouse.com | Moderate*

CARLTON ATLANTIC COAST HOTEL

Most ⚹ rooms boast fabulous views of the harbour. All creature comforts, swimming pool, spa, a fine restaurant. *85 rooms | Coast Road (The Quay) | tel. 098 29 00 | www.atlanticcoasthotel.com | Expensive*

THE WYATT

Older, typically Irish hotel with a bright yellow frontage and view of Westport's central square. Often live music in the bar. *52 rooms | The Octagon | tel. 098 25 027 | www.wyatthotel.com | Moderate*

INFORMATION

TOURIST INFORMATION OFFICE
James' Street | tel. 098 25 711 | www.westporttourism.com

WHERE TO GO

ACHILL ISLAND (128 A1) (*ſ B9*)

For many, the country's largest island is no longer a true island as it has been con-

Many pilgrims and hikers head up Ireland's holy mountain, conical Croagh Patrick

nected to the mainland by a swing bridge since 1888. On Atlantic Drive, the stretch between Cloughmore and Dooega offers up magnificent views of a harsh nature with bog and heather landscapes, spectacular cliffs and beautiful sandy beaches. It was on this island – some 12 miles long and 13.5 miles wide – that German Nobel Prize-winning author Heinrich Böll wrote his *Irish Journal*. Böll's former residence in Dugort is today used by international artists as a creative retreat.

While the island, with a population of under 3000, can seem fairly desolate in winter, in summer the few guesthouses and hotels fill up quickly. Visitors keen on staying at Keel Bay in the west near Achill Head (with the turquoise waters of charming Keem beach), should book ahead. The island's water sports centre is particularly popular with windsurfers. *www.goachill.com*

CROAGH PATRICK ⚡
(128 B2) *(𝄢 C10)*

The best starting point for climbing the 2,500-ft conical mountain 5.5 miles southwest of Westport is *Murrisk Abbey*, an Augustinian friary on the bay, dating back to 1457. The small chapel on the summit yields fabulous panoramic views all the way to Achill Island.

It is said that in the year 441 Saint Patrick fasted up here for 40 days. Since then the mountain has been a pilgrimage destination for the Irish, particularly on the last Sunday in July. Legend tells how Patrick rang his bell to attract all the snakes in Ireland, who fell to their death into the abyss, thus freeing the country from snakes for all times. From *Murrisk*, with a statue of St Patrick slightly above the friary, it will take you about two hours to ascend to the summit, but watch the loose scree towards the top.

The *visitor centre* is open between March and Oct, offering crafts and a restaurant alongside information *(www.croagh-patrick.com)*.

NEWPORT (128 B1) *(𝄢 C9)*

The road leads north along Clew Bay to Newport (8 mi). The route is manageable by bike, being the only one around Westport not involving hills. Look out for a 19th-century railway bridge that was part of a former railway service from Achill Island via Newport to Westport with onwards connection to Dublin. And don't miss *Carrickhowley Castle* 3 miles outside Newport. The tower house dating back to the 16th century with round corner towers used to belong to the Pirate Queen Grace O'Malley (1530–1603). In Ireland, numerous ballads keep alive the memory of this daughter of a clan chief and worthy adversary of Queen Elizabeth I.

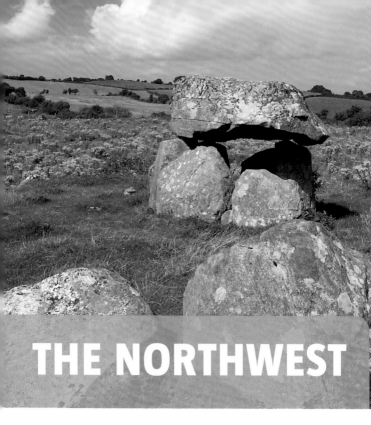

THE NORTHWEST

Donegal and Sligo, the two northern-most counties in Ireland, are dominated by mountainous landscapes, fine sandy beaches, numerous lakes and jagged coastlines.

Even if the sun can sometimes plays hard-to-get here, Donegal and Sligo have a charm all their own, made up of rugged yet sublime landscapes. Wherever you go you will encounter testimonies to the past, such as the remains of a prehistoric cult of the dead at the tombs of *Carrowmore* – probably the oldest prehistoric burial places in Ireland – and Bronze Age stone circles.

In west Donegal, Gaelic customs and language are still widespread. Unemployment is a major issue here; there

are not enough jobs left in traditional agriculture or in the tweed mills. However, more resources are being made available for tourism, and there is now a direct flight from Dublin to Carrickfinn in the west of Donegal.

SLIGO

(125 E5) *(Ø E8)* **The small port of Sligo (pop. 20,000) on the estuary of the Garavogue River in Sligo Bay lies at the heart of Ireland's northwest.**

County Sligo, a region full of mountains, lakes, forests and rivers, was home to the poet W B Yeats. The Nobel Prize winner called it *The Land of Heart's Desire* and

Photo: Dolmen in Carrowmore

From Sligo to Donegal: in the northwest of the country, the Irish language and traditional customs are still upheld

immortalised the mythic beauties of the region in the drama of that name as a literary monument.

Everywhere you go in town, buildings and inscriptions commemorate the poet who grew up in Sligo. The annual INSIDER TIP *Yeats International Summer School* in August attracts over 200 students and professors from all over the world. This place of Yeatsian pilgrimage offers devotees inspiring seminars, lectures, walks and evening chats in the pubs. Another site of pilgrimage for numerous Yeats fans is the island of *Innisfree* south of Sligo in Lough Gill, immortalised in a Yeats poem.

In summer, Sligo wakes up from its provincial slumber; the streets fill with people strolling, pubs and shops remain open until late at night. Rising temperatures bring about a near-Mediterranean atmosphere. It's worth scheduling a stopover in Sligo if only for the substantial number of cosy pubs. One of the most

Rosses Point: meeting place for deep-sea anglers and windsurfers

SLIGO COUNTY MUSEUM ★

What lies behind the special magic of Sligo? This small museum tries to find an answer: Sligo's millennia-old dolmens (burial sites constructed from stone blocks) and mystic stone circles are presented as original stones and illustrations in a quantity unrivalled elsewhere in the British Isles. The other focal point is, surprise, surprise, William Butler Yeats, with photographs and newspaper cuttings. The poet's Nobel Prize medal is also on show. The art gallery shows Expressionistic landscape paintings by his younger brother Jack Butler Yeats, who was one of Ireland's most important 20th-century artists. *June–Sept Tue–Sat 10am–noon, 2–5pm, Oct–May Tue–Sat 2–5pm | free admission | Stephen Street*

YEATS MEMORIAL BUILDING

William Butler Yeats, poet, dramatist and critic, was bon on 13 June 1865 in Dublin and grew up in Sligo. Yeats is one of the most-anthologised lyricists of modern times, receiving the Nobel Prize for Literature in 1923. For a long while Yeats lived in this pretty building, erected by his grandfather. *Mon–Sat 9am–5pm | free admission | Hyde Bridge, O'Connell Street, corner of Wine Street | www.yeats-sligo.com*

beautiful has been around for 150 years: **INSIDER TIP** *Hargadon's (4/5 O'Connell Street, Sligo | tel. 071 9 15 37 09 | www.hargadons.com)* is a gem with flagstone floors, traditional turf fire and separate wood-panelled booths.

Sligo is also a popular starting point for tours of several days into Donegal, Ireland's northernmost county.

SIGHTSEEING

SLIGO ABBEY

Over the course of the centuries, the 13th-century Dominican monastery suffered severe damage several times. The ruins still have a strong atmosphere. There is a cloister, and tombstones from the Gothic and Renaissance periods lie on a meadow. Look out for the fine stonemasonry work on a 15th-century high altar. *April–Oct daily 10am–6pm | admission 3 euros | Abbey Street*

FOOD & DRINK

AUSTIES RESTAURANT & BAR

Austie's serves mainly fish specialities and seafood from the Atlantic, as well as traditional Irish lamb dishes. Vegetarians are catered for too. *Rosses Point | tel. 071 9 17 71 11 | Moderate*

BISTRO BIANCONI

For many, this is the best Italian restaurant in Ireland: crispy pizzas, lasagne and various pasta dishes. On a budget?

Go for the 'early bird' afternoon dinner. Very popular, especially at the weekend. *Daily 12.30–2.30pm and from 5.30pm onwards | 44 O'Connell Street | tel. 071 9 14 17 44 | www.bistrobianconi.ie | Moderate*

CONRAD'S KITCHEN

Star chef Conrad Gallagher, who has already cooked for guests of state at the White House in Washington, opened this trendy restaurant in 2010. Try *roasted scallops with butternut squash* and other gourmet dishes for relatively reasonable prices. *Closed Mon | The Model, The Mall | tel. 071 9 14 14 05 | www.conradskitchen. com | Moderate*

FIDDLERS CREEK

This welcoming cross between a pub and rustic restaurant serves inexpensive classics such as *chicken wings or garlic mushrooms* in the bar, then for dinner tortilla, steaks or exotically refined specialities such as salmon in a ginger-lime sauce. *Rockwood Parade | tel. 071 9 14 18 66 | www.fiddlerscreek.ie | Moderate*

SHOPPING

MICHAEL KENNEDY CERAMICS

Vases, candlesticks, bowls, most of them in a strong purple colour – the artist is known all over the country for his designs inspired by Irish nature. *Market Cross | Market Street | www.michaelkennedy ceramics.com*

LEISURE & SPORTS

KILCULLEN'S SEAWEED BATHS

Since 1912 people have taken baths here, once in order to combat rheumatism and arthritis, today to fight stress, cellulite and a Guinness hangover. Seawater and the iodine-rich oils oozing out of the seaweed are the miracle remedy. *Daily 10am–8pm | 25 euros | Pier Road Inishscrone (Enniscrone) | tel. 096 3 62 38 | www.kilcullensseaweedbaths.com*

ROSSES POINT

Meeting place for deep-sea anglers and windsurfers; the clean beaches are an added bonus. *Details from the tourist information*

SLIGO RIDING SCHOOL

The riding centre (2.5 m away) offers beach rides or trail rides into the nearby hills and forests. Tuition takes place in a large covered arena and an outside paddock. You can choose to stay longer, for a package with accommodation, hacks and tuition. *Carrowmore | tel. 087 2 30 48 28 | www.irelandonhorseback.com*

MARCO POLO HIGHLIGHTS

⭐ **Sligo County Museum**
Memorabilia and more: a fascinating presentation of the life and times of William Butler Yeats → p. 82

⭐ **Carrowmore**
Hiking between burial chambers: a megalithic cemetery and the grave of Queen Maeve → p. 85

⭐ **Giant's Causeway**
It is said that a giant carried thousands of hexagonal basalt columns – for love → p. 86

⭐ **Lough Derg**
The charming inland lake turns into a pilgrimage site in summer – and is an all-year-round bird sanctuary → p. 87

INSIDER TIP VOYA SEAWEED BATHS ●

Taking a bath in slimy seaweed used to be an Irish tradition – at the beginning of the 20th century, there were still hundreds of bath houses. Today, detoxifying seaweed baths are back in fashion. Massages and full-body wraps are on offer too – in an attractive luxurious ambience. *Mon–Tue noon–8pm, Wed–Fri 11am–8pm, Sat/Sun 10am–8pm | 25 euros/50 min | Strandhill | tel. 071 9 16 86 86 | www.celticseaweedbaths.com*

ENTERTAINMENT

HAWK'S WELL THEATRE

This small theatre puts on mainly Irish plays. *Temple Street | tel. 071 9 16 15 18 | www.hawkswell.com*

INSIDER TIP SHEELA-NA-GIG (FUREY'S)

Typically Irish pub, popular with the locals. Three to four times a week traditional live music, Wednesdays jazz evening. *Bridge Street*

LOW BUDGET

▶ Inexpensive accommodation at the *Harbour House*: today, the old residence of the harbourmaster is a hostel. It is only 5 minutes walk into the town centre and the bus/train station. *48 beds | Finisklin Road, Sligo | tel. 071 9 17 15 47 | www.harbourhousehostel.com*

▶ Fancy surfing the tempting waves at Strandhill? Get yourself a used board from *Outer Point | Lockwood Parade, Sligo (behind Hyde Bridge), tel. 071 9 14 69 50*

WHERE TO STAY

SLIGO CITY HOTEL

The redbrick building with clocktower and granite portico offers well-kept rooms (incl. tea and coffee-making facilities) in a top central location, as well as an in-house restaurant and pub. *60 rooms | Quay Street | tel. 071 9 14 40 00 | www.sligocityhotel.com | Moderate*

SLIGO SOUTHERN HOTEL

The elegant façade hides large rooms, a high level of comfort – and Finnegan's Bar. *98 rooms | Strandhill Road | tel. 071 9 16 21 01 | www.sligosouthernhotel.com | Expensive*

INSIDER TIP TEMPLE HOUSE

Extensive country estate amidst pastures and forests. The guest rooms are furnished with antique furniture. The many activities on offer include horse riding and fishing. *6 rooms | April–Nov | Ballymote (a good 12 mi south of Sligo) | tel. 071 9 18 33 29 | www.templehouse.ie | Moderate*

INFORMATION

TOURIST OFFICE

Temple, corner of Charles Street | tel. 071 9 16 12 01 | www.irelandnorthwest.ie

WHERE TO GO

BALLYSHANNON (125 E4) (𝄞 F7)

The pretty little town (pop. 2800) on the estuary of the River Erne is the birthplace of the late musician Rory Gallagher, who was born here in 1948 at the Rock(!) Hospital and became one of the best guitarists on the European music scene of the 1970s. To commemorate the blues-rock legend who died in 1995, many bands find their way to Ballyshannon *(early*

June | www.goingtomyhometown.com)
for the INSIDER TIP ▶ *Rory Gallagher International Tribute Festival*.

Visitors preferring a less rocky visit appreciate the two potteries of national fame, as well as pretty craft shops. It's also worth timing your visit to coincide with the *Music Festival* (first weekend of August), a showcase of traditional Irish music, attracting well-known performers as well as newcomers.

BUNDORAN (125 E4) *(ᗅ F7)*

Taking the N 15 in the direction of Donegal takes you past Drumcliffe, the site of W. B. Yeats' grave, to the sea resort of Bundoran (pop. 1800). The sandy beaches are good for water sports of all kinds, while golfers too enjoy coming here. Adults can take surf lessons or join a fishing trip, children will enjoy the leisure pool complex. Accommodation with sea view in the traditional *Fitzgerald's Hotel* (16 rooms | Main Road | tel. 071 9 84 13 36 | www.fitzgeraldshotel.com | *Moderate*).

CARROWMORE ★
(125 E5) *(ᗅ E8)*

Carrowmore (2.5 mi southwest of Sligo) boasts the second-largest megalithic cemetery in Europe. The complex was set up in approx. 3850 BC, long before the Celts came to Ireland, and is even older than Newgrange! Stroll amongst the remains of dolmens, stone circles and burial chambers, and climb the nearby mountain of *Knocknarea* (there is a signposted *Chambered Cairn* trail from Sligo)! The cairn on top of the ☀ summit is said to be the last resting place of Queen Maeve. Tradition has it that the belligerent Maeve – a central figure of Irish mythology – was buried standing up and in full armour. *Easter–Oct daily 10am–6pm | admission 2.10 euros*

DONEGAL (125 F3) *(ᗅ F7)*

40 miles northeast of Sligo, Donegal (pop. 2300) lies on the estuary where the Eske River runs into Donegal Bay. The centre of the town is formed by a large triangular square called *The Diamond*, as is the custom in the northern parts of

Donegal Castle occupies a dominant position square above a river near the market

the country; this is also where the traffic arteries from Sligo, Derry and West Donegal converge. The 8-metre obelisk commemorates four Franciscan priests, whose ruined abbey (1474) can be seen at the estuary south of town.

The square is the starting point for a sign-posted *walking tour*, leading past various sights, including *Donegal Castle*. Built in the 15th century by the O'Donnell dynasty, today's buildings date mostly from the 17th century *(March–Oct daily 10am–6pm | admission 4 euros)*. For accommodation with excellent restaurant look no further than the *Central Hotel* (112 rooms | tel. 074 9 72 10 27 | www. centralhoteldonegal.com | *Moderate*)

84 | 85

with a pretty view of the square, the river and the bay. *Tourist information in Quay Street | tel. 074 9 72 11 48 | www. donegaldirect.ie*

GIANT'S CAUSEWAY ★
(126 127 C–D 1) (*ⱷ J5*)

From Donegal, a drive of almost 90 miles via Londonderry/Derry leads to Northern Ireland's main attraction: over 38,000 hexagonal basalt columns jutting out of the wind-whipped ocean. Numerous myths surround the creation of the basalt columns. The most beautiful story tells how giant Finn MacCool fell madly in love with a young girl who lived on a remote island in the Hebrides. In order to get to his beloved without getting his feet wet, Finn created this stony path. Scientists reckon that the Giant's Causeway was formed over 60 million years ago, when lava breaking through the earth's crust solidified.

Starting point for a hike along the natural formation, almost two miles north of Bushmills, is *Portballintrae*. From the *visitor centre (daily 10am–5pm)* a path leads to the coast (15 min). Before turning right for the Causeway, look out for *Camel Rock* jutting out of the water in Portnaboe Bay. A bit further on, rock formation with evocative names. The *Wishing Chair* for instance does suggest the form of a stone chair. At the *Organ* the near-vertical basalt columns jut up into the skies up to 15 m. From here, the

Ireland as it used to be: village history brought to life at Glencolumbkille

Shepherd's Path leads onto the cliffs of the *Aird Snout* mountain. Nearby *Bushmills* is well worth a detour: the famous whiskey distillery is the world's oldest. *April–Oct Mon–Sat 9am–5pm, Sun noon–5pm, Nov–March Mon–Fri 10.30am–3.30pm, Sun 1.30–3.30pm | admission 6 euros | www.bushmills.com*

INSIDER TIP GLENCOLUMBKILLE
(125 D3) (*Ø E7*)

At the end of a lonely mountain valley, the village of Glencolumbkille boasts a very proactive international Irish-language college *(wwwo.oideas-gael.com)*. At the nearby *Folk Village Museum*, hourly tours lead through three cottages furnished in the original style from the time between 1700 to 1900. A school, a pub, a craft shop as well as a teashop complete the historical village *(35 mi west of Donegal | Easter–Sept Mon–Sat 10am–6pm, Sun noon–6pm, Oct Mon–Fri 11am–3pm | admission 5 euros | www. glenfolkvillage.com)*. On the way back it's well worth detouring to *Slieve League*, at 1968 ft the highest sea cliffs in Europe.

LOUGH DERG ★ (125 F3–4) (*Ø F7*)

Mystic sites of faith: several islets lie at the centre of Lough Derg, an elongated lake surrounded by small villages, about 9 miles southeast of Donegal. Holy Island was the site of a 7th-century monastic settlement that is shrouded in myth (in the summer months, boat trips across can be organised from the harbour). Discover Early Christian tombstones, hermitage cells and four archaic chapels.

For over a thousand years, *Station Island* has been a European site of pilgrimage. According to legend, St Patrick spent 40 days here praying and fasting. During the pilgrimage season between June and August, the island may only be visited by believers. These stay three days and three nights, their only sustenance black tea and toast. One-day (silent) retreats are also on offer; even families are given the opportunity for some inner contemplation. *www.loughderg.org*

LOUGH GILL (125 E5) (*Ø E–F8*)

From Sligo, a 22-mile drive leads around Lough Gill, a picturesque lake amidst wooded hills. Leaving Sligo on the N 16, turn right onto the R 286, following signs to *Hazelwood Estate*. A side road brings you to *Half Moon Bay* (picnic site), the starting point for hikes along the lake and through the adjoining woods. Back on the R 286, you reach *Parke's Castle*, a romantic-looking 17th-century fort *(April–Sept 10am–6pm | admission 3 euros)*. At the entrance to the village of Dromahair, a path leads to the Franciscan monastery of *Creevylea Abbey* of 1508. The path following on from there leads away from the lake, only joining up with it again at *Dooney Rock Forest*. An information brochure on the beautiful *nature trail* along the lake shore can be picked up at the car park.

ROSSES POINT (125 E5) (*Ø E8*)

Located almost three miles northwest of Sligo, this village boasts the *County Sligo Golf Club (tel. 071 9 17 71 34 | www.county sligogolfclub.ie)*, considered by many to be the most beautiful golf course in Ireland. Sun worshippers swear by the long sandy beaches and small beach bars.

STRANDHILL (125 E5) (*Ø E8*)

This popular holiday village lies on the coast (approx. 5 mi west of Sligo). While it is a popular surfing beach, swimming can be dangerous here: look out for lifeguards and flags. Sligo's airport is also near Strandhill, offering sightseeing flights with light aircraft alongside daily services to Dublin.

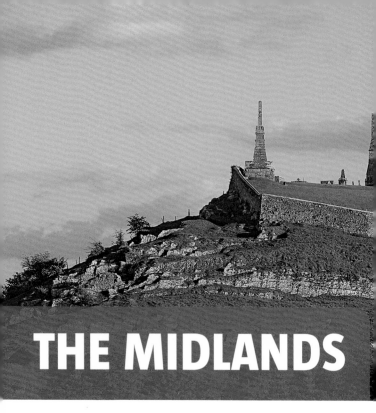

THE MIDLANDS

Rainbows over gentle hills, wide plains and friendly villages: Ireland's heartland between Dublin und Galway is dominated by small lakes and numerous reminders of the Christian culture, of such significance for Ireland.

If you're looking to spend a calm holiday visiting cafés and going for long walks and boat tours, you have come to the right place. There is also a medieval gem just waiting to be discovered in the Midlands: Kilkenny will conquer any visitor's heart.

Thanks to careful urban planning Kilkenny's historic heritage was kept intact. Colourful façades and centuries-old pubs, winding alleyways, traditional shops and the splendid complex of Kilkenny Castle on the river Nore as a landmark make the charm of a city that is also the capital of the eponymous county. In the Middle Ages, Kilkenny even became the unofficial capital of Ireland with its own Anglo-Norman parliament. The urban and cultural heritage of that era, as well as the idyllic surroundings, are best explored by bike.

KILKENNY

(135 D2) (*H14*)   **Picture-postcard Ireland: Kilkenny (pop. 26,000) is the best-preserved medieval city in Ireland.**

SIGHTSEEING

BLACK ABBEY CHURCH
In the carefully restored abbey, a Dominican church founded around 1225, Holy

---

Photo: Rock of Cashel with cathedral

The cradle of Christianity: numerous ruins are a reminder of the region's many monasteries

Mass is still said on a daily basis. Look out for an architectural gem: the lead-glazed rosary window consisting of five vertical segments featuring the mysteries of the rosary – particularly beautiful when the sun shines through in glory. *Daily 8am–6pm | Abbey Street*

KILKENNY CASTLE ⭐

Built in 1190, the Norman fortification served as the family seat of the influential Butler family until 1967. Charging the symbolic sum of 50 pounds, Arthur Butler gave the crumbling castle to the Irish state, which started a comprehensive emergency restoration programme. Today, Kilkenny's iconic landmark is resplendent again, presenting numerous attractions. A 45-minute guided tour shows valuable antique furniture as well as oil paintings of the Butler clan in the Long Gallery. The lower floor houses the *Butler Gallery (www.butlergallery.com | free admission)*, one of the Ireland's foremost galleries for contemporary and modern art. *April–Sept 9.30am–*

*5.30pm, Oct–March 9.30am–4.30pm |
admission 6 euros | Castle Street | www.
kilkennycastle.ie*

ROTHE HOUSE

Kilkenny's regional museum is housed in three burghers' houses in the Tudor style, one behind the other. These buildings, erected between 1594 and 1610,

SHEE ALMS HOUSE

The Tudor house built in 1582 by Sir Richard Shee houses the *Tourist Information Centre*. Behind the grey quarry-stone walls, the prosperous Shee merchant family accommodated old, sick and poor citizens: the almshouse performed its charitable duty up until 1830. *Rose Inn Street*

Colourful houses and centuries-old pubs: Kilkenny is a great place for ambling around

alone are worth a visit. 18th-century paintings, antique furniture and historic exhibits from the region are presented in the white-washed rooms with pretty oak-beam ceilings. An insider tip for garden lovers is the adjoining *Rothe Garden*, laid out in 17th-century style, in which kitchen herbs, fruit trees and flowers from traditional peasant gardens thrive. *April–Oct Mon–Sat 10.30am–5pm, Sun 3–5pm, Nov–March Mon–Sat 10.30am–4.30pm | admission 5 euros | Parliament Street | www.rothehouse.com*

ST CANICE'S CATHEDRAL

Dating back to the 13th century, the interior of the church houses a number of 16th-century tombs featuring reliefs in black marble. A nearly 100-ft round tower next to the church is the only remnant of an early monastic settlement. *June–Aug Mon–Sat 9am–6pm, Sun 2–6pm, Sept–May Mon–Sat 10am–1pm and 2–5pm, Sun 2–5pm | admission 4 euros | Church Lane | www.stcanices cathedral.com*

FOOD & DRINK

CAFÉ SOL
Fresh ingredients, friendly service: café-restaurant opposite the Tholsel (town hall) serving Irish-Mediterranean fare. *William St. | tel. 056 776 49 87 | www.cafesolkilkenny.com | Moderate*

KILKENNY SHOP RESTAURANT
Coffee shop in the *Kilkenny Design Centre* opposite Kilkenny Castle serving delicious snacks. *Daily 10am–5pm | Castle Yard | Moderate*

KYTELER'S INN
Restaurant dating back to the 14th century. Dame Alice Kyteler is said to have lived here once. When Dame Alice was accused of witchcraft, she vamoosed, leaving her old maidservant to take the blame. Pretty courtyard with two fountains. *Daily from midday | Kieran Street | tel. 056 772 10 64 | www.kytelersinn.ie | Expensive*

PORDYLO'S
This stone building dates back to the 16th century. Specialities: fish, crustaceans, game. *Butterslip Lane, corner of High Street | tel. 056 777 06 60 | Expensive*

RISTORANTE RINUCCINI
An Irish-Italian couple combining refined with rustic cuisine – unsurpassable. *1 The Parade, opposite the Castle | tel. 056 776 15 75 | www.rinuccini.com | Moderate*

SHOPPING

KILKENNY DESIGN CENTRE ★
Happy to experiment, the artists in their workshops in the former mews of Kilkenny Castle are always developing new designs from materials such as ceramics, gold and silver, glass, wood and wool. Popular souvenirs, alongside fancy Barbour waxed garments, are woollen wares from Donegal of the *Fishermen out of Ireland brand*. After all this browsing, enjoy an Irish snack in the adjacent atmospheric *Castleyard Café* with a view of the cobblestone yard of Kilkenny Castle. *Castle Yard, off Castle Road | Mon–Sat 9am–6pm, Sun from 10am | www.kilkennydesign.com*

ENTERTAINMENT

EDWARD LANGTON BAR & RESTAURANT
Stylish rustic atmosphere; the hotel bar has received the 'Pub of the Year' garland a few times already. *69 John Street | www.langtons.ie*

MARCO POLO HIGHLIGHTS

★ **Kilkenny Castle**
Wonderfully preserved medieval stronghold → p. 89

★ **Kilkenny Design Centre**
Pioneer of Irish craft design → p. 91

★ **Carrick-on-Suir**
Pretty small town on the river Suir → p. 93

★ **Rock of Cashel**
The elevated plateau with the famous cathedral was the seat of kings and a site of St Patrick's miracle work → p. 93

★ **Dunmore Cave**
Imposing stalactite cave with many long corridors, where evidence was found of a Viking attack 1000 years ago → p. 95

Gigantic construction: the telescope at Birr Castle, dating back to 1840, is still functional

WHERE TO STAY

BUTLER HOUSE

Hiding behind the façade, festooned with creepers, of the former residence of 18th-century Lady Eleanor Butler, puristically elegant and individually styled rooms and suites await. To partake of the exquisite breakfast, walk through the garden of the manor house into the rooms of the former Kilkenny stables. *13 rooms | 16 Patrick Street | tel. 056 772 28 28 | www.butler.ie | Moderate*

GLENDINE INN

The 250-year-old pub, a 20-minute walk from the city centre, offers en-suite rooms. *7 rooms | Castlecomer Road | tel. 056 772 10 69 | www.glendineinn.com | Budget*

KILKENNY RIVER COURT ✼

Four-star hotel with swimming pool, gym and a splendid view across the river to Kilkenny Castle. The large rooms are furnished in country style, the three-course lunch in the *Riverside Restaurant* is a local institution. Unsurpassed however is afternoon tea in the sunshine on the terrace of the *Riverview Bar. 90 rooms | The Bridge, off John Street | tel. 056 772 33 88 | www.rivercourthotel.com | Expensive*

ZUNI

Chic and sophisticated: the building, opened in 1902 as Kilkenny's first theatre, today houses an extraordinary boutique hotel. Equally renowned is the in-house restaurant serving Maria Raferty's modern Irish cuisine to island-wide acclaim. *13 rooms | 26 Patrick Street | tel. 056 772 39 99 | www.zuni.ie | Moderate–Expensive*

INFORMATION

TOURIST OFFICE

Shee Alms House | Rose Inn Street | tel. 056 775 15 00 | www.kilkennytourism.ie

WHERE TO GO

BIRR (129 F4) (*ℳ F12*)

Some 44 miles northwest, the small town of Birr (pop. 5000) boasts fabulous green spaces such as the *Millennium Gardens* (belonging to the Earls of Rosse), the country's largest, as well as a castle with a INSIDER TIP historic telescope. From 1840 onwards, the third Earl of Rosse dedicated over 70 years to building the world's largest telescope (which by the way still works!). His son was able to correctly determine the temperature of the moon *(daily 9am–6pm | admission 9 euros | www.birrcastle.com)*. Accommodation options include *Doolys Hotel,* a 250-year-old coach station on the town's Georgian central square, with a good restaurant *(18 rooms | Emmet Square | tel. 057 9 12 00 32 | www.doolyshotel.com | Moderate)*.

CAHIR (134 B3) (ᗕ *F15*)

Erected in the 13th century in the pretty village of Cahir (44 miles southwest), situated on a small rocky island in the river Suir, the stronghold of Cahir Castle was extended and remodelled several times up to the 19th century. Under the Earls of Ormond, the impregnable castle developed into one of the most powerful in the country *(daily 9.30am–5.30pm | admission 3 euros)*. Accommodation is available for instance at the *Cahir House Hotel (41 rooms | The Square | tel. 052 7 44 30 00 | www.cahirhousehotel.ie | Moderate)*. In a stone house belonging to the old mill, the INSIDER TIP *Galileo Café (Church Street, near Craft Canary | tel. 052 7 44 56 89 | Budget–Moderate)* serves up Italian-Mediterranean fare; bring your own wine. Almost two miles southeast of town on a hill in Kilcommon southeast of town, discover *Swiss Cottage*, a splendid thatched wooden house with 19th-century dormer windows *(in summer daily 10am–6pm, Nov/ March/April Tue–Sun 10am–1pm, 2–5pm | admission 2.90 euros | access via Caher Wood and Ardfinnan Road, R 670)*.

CARRICK-ON-SUIR ★
(134 C3) (ᗕ *G15*)

The main attraction in the little town (pop. 6000, 25 miles south) is ● *Ormond Castle* (1560), a castle-like Elizabethan manor house next to two 15th-century inhabitable defensive towers *(April*

–Sept daily 10am–6pm | free admission). The medieval stone bridge across the the river Suir is worth a look too. The *Heritage Centre* on Main Street shows local finds, historic photographs and the 17th-century church silver belonging to the Earl of Ormond. *(Mon–Fri 10am–5pm, in summer also Sat | free admission)*.

CASHEL (134 B3) (ᗕ *F14*)

The most important sight in this little town (pop. 3200), a good 30 miles west on the N 8, is the imposing ★ *Rock of Cashel*. The Celts in their day already worshipped the rock, on which subsequently a cathedral (13th century), a chapel and a round tower were built. According to legend, it was here that St Patrick explained the Holy Trinity using a shamrock leaf – marking the birth of an Irish icon *(March–May daily 9.30am–5pm, June–Sept 9am–7pm, Oct–Feb 9.30am–4pm |*

LOW BUDGET

▶ The *Kilkenny Tourist Hostel*, a Georgian townhouse, offers good-value rooms. *60 beds in 11 rooms | 35 Parliament Street | tel. 056 7 76 35 41 | www.kilkennyhostel.ie*

▶ Want to save the entrance fee for *Kilkenny Castle*? Take a free stroll through the park and visit the castle's in-house Butler Gallery of Modern Art *(www.butlergallery.com)*.

▶ The *Brú Ború* arts centre at the foot of the Rock of Cashel puts on traditional music, folkdancing, performances and readings *(June–Sept | tel. 062 6 11 22 | www.comhaltas.ie)*; charges are either non-existent or low.

admission 5.30 euros). The *Cashel Folk Village* on Dominick Street consists of re-constructions of thatched village shops and a chapel *(March/April daily 10am–6pm, May–Oct daily 9.30am–7.30pm | admission 4 euros)*, while the *Cashel Heritage Centre* shows a model of the town in the year 1640 *(City Hall | March–Oct daily 9.30am–5.30pm, Nov–Feb Mon–Fri 9.30am–5.30pm | free admission | www.cashel.ie)*. The INSIDER TIP *Cashel Palace Hotel*, former residence of the archbishop, has been turned into a picture-postcard country house: featuring marble fireplaces, oak parquet flooring and views of gardens or the Rock of Cashel *(23 rooms | Main Street | tel. 062/627 07 | www.cashel-palace.ie | Expensive)*.

CLONMACNOISE (129 F3–4) (*ⓘ F11*)

Even on gloomy days, the ecclesiastical ruins, high crosses and a 62-ft round tower exude a powerful charm all their own. From 548 onwards, a community of monks found shelter in the abbey founded by the hermit Ciaran (Kieran). For nearly a millennium, the ecclesiastical and spiritual elite of the island lived in Clonmacnoise (74 miles northwest on the River Shannon). Every year on 9 September, a pilgrimage takes place here. *Daily 10am–6pm | admission 6 euros*

CLONMEL (134 C3) (*ⓘ G15*)

A good 30 miles southwest, discover the charming small town of Clonmel (pop. 17,000). Why not visit the *South Tip-*

BOOKS & FILMS

▶ **Irish Journal** – Thousands followed in the footsteps of Nobel-Prize winner Heinrich Böll to Achill Island, an island off the west coast, where he had a holiday home. Hugo Hamilton's **The Island of Talking** is a wonderfully insightful exploration of Böll's world and the Irish psyche.

▶ **The Secret Scripture** – Sebastian Barry's moving and unsentimental novel, told in two perspectives that join in a clever twist at the end

▶ **McCarthy's Bar** – The late British TV comedian Pete McCarthy visits the country of his parents

▶ **Once** – The independent film by John Carney (2007), a love story between a busker and an immigrant, was awarded an Oscar for Best Song

▶ **Angela's Ashes** – the late Frank McCourt's childhood memories of life in the slums of Limerick won the Pulitzer Prize and was turned into a major film (2000) by Alan Parker

▶ **Ulysses** – James Joyce reports the minutiae of a single day (16 June 1904) in the life of Leopold Bloom, advertising agent of a Dublin newspaper – the novel is considered a milestone of modern fiction

▶ **Round Ireland in Low Gear** – Hilarious: classic British travel writer Eric Newby recounting his bike tours through the country

▶ **The Wind that shakes the Barley** – the film tells the story of the Irish fight for independence post-1916, winning Ken Loach the 2006 Palme d'Or

Popular activity: exploring the Shannon region by houseboat

perary County Museum (*Mick Delahunty Square | Tue–Sat 10am–5pm | free admission*), which uses changing exhibitions to document the history of the county since prehistoric times, as well as the *Friary*.

DUNMORE CAVE ★ (135 D2) (*⌖ H13*)

It's only 7.5 miles to the north (*Castlecomer*) on the N 78 from Kilkenny to this massive limestone cave. The cave was the place of refuge chosen in 928 by people fleeing a Viking attack – it turned into a death trap: they were smoked out by their pursuers. During excavations in 1973, the remains of 44 people were discovered, mostly women and children. The cave is well-lit; just as well, with the steep descent into the widespread network of underground corridors. Down below cavities full of stalactites, stalagmites and columns await, amongst them the 7-metre *Market Cross,* Europe's largest free-standing stalagmite. *June–Sept daily 9.30am–6.30pm, March–May, Oct 10am–5pm | admission 3 euros*

JERPOINT ABBEY (135 D3) (*⌖ H14*)

The former Cistercian monastery 16 miles south of Kilkenny dates back to the 12th century. The building, entirely built from stone with a crenellated rectangular defensive tower, boasts rich figurative ornamentation in the 14th-century cloisters. *Thomastown | Oct, March–May daily 10am–5pm, June–Sept 10am–6pm, Nov 10am–4pm | admission 3 euros*

SHANNON RIVER
(128 –129 C–D6) (*⌖ C–D14*)

The longest river in the country (nearly 250 miles) forms numerous large lakes between its Lough Allen source and the city of Limerick. A popular leisure activity is tours with houseboats or cabin cruisers on the river, its lakes and the Grand Canal, branching off towards Dublin. *www. river-shannon.com*

SLIEVE BLOOM MOUNTAINS
(132 B5) (*⌖ G12*)

An ideal area for easy hikes (37 miles northwest of Kilkenny), such as the ☆ *Ard Erin*, only 1998 ft high. For a good 18 miles, the *Slieve Bloom Way* leads through forests and along moorland. A good starting point for the tour is *Glen Barrow,* southwest of Rosenallis. A stylish choice of accommodation is *Roundwood House* near Mountrath, a pretty *bed & breakfast (10 rooms | tel. 057 8 73 21 20 | www.roundwoodhouse. com | Moderate).*

TRIPS & TOURS

① ON THE DINGLE WAY BETWEEN TRALEE AND DINGLE BAY

🚶 The northernmost peninsula in the south of Ireland is Dingle. The 111-mile Dingle Way long-distance trail covers nearly the entire peninsula. Particularly beautiful is the section of approx. 35 mi between Tralee and Dingle, for which you should plan three days with 7 to 8 hours' walking each.

This hike, with ascents of up to 1115 feet, leads you on mountain trails and through fern-covered valleys, along clear brooks, and offers repeated views across Tralee Bay and Dingle Bay. From Tralee, head in a southwesterly direction towards Blennerville. For just over a mile the none-too-demanding trail leads along the bank of the former Tralee Ship Canal of 1846, today mostly silted up and harbouring swans and other waterfowl. Here, the Dingle Way forms part of the North Kerry Way. Don't miss the old sluice gates at the harbour. This is where many Irish boarded the boat to America in the 19th century. A tourist attraction is the 200-year-old windmill of Blennerville, beautifully restored and still working today – the largest in the British Isles. Grouped around the mill are an exhibition centre, craft shops and a restaurant *(Blennerville Windmill and Museum | June–Aug daily 9am–6pm, April/May and Sept/Oct daily 9.30am–*

Photo: Dingle peninsula, Clogher Head

A lonely coast, wild trails, historic towns and a gentle boat tour down the stream: experience Ireland close-up

5.30pm | admission 5 euros). While the historical steam train between Tralee and Blennerville is not currently running, Tralee is on bus and train routes and Blennerville can be reached by bus. From Blennerville, quiet country roads (single-lane, asphalted) lead south, gently ascending to **Tonavane** on the slopes of the Slieve Mish Mountains. On the old country road to Dingle you are walking on the historically most interesting part of the section. From Tonavane onwards

hiking becomes more difficult: it is a stony path that leads to **Killelton** under 7 miles away. The adventurous trail runs over old wooden bridges and over stepping stones to cross brooks, and across open mountain scenery with views of Tralee Bay; it is only just before Killelton that the trail is paved again. In **Killelton**, a village abandoned in the 19th century, you can find the remnants of the **St Elton Oratory** overgrown with ivy and fuchsia. The Early Christian oratory dates back to

about 1.5 hours from road level and is a bit strenuous; carry on and think of the reward: fantastic views across the sea and the Dingle Peninsula.

The next morning, the Dingle Way carries on southwest across the peninsula, taking you past extended boggy plains where peat is still cut. Towards the south the latter part of the day affords spectacular panoramic views towards Dingle Bay. On a clear day you can see the jagged mountain scenery of the neighbouring Iveragh Peninsula from here. Finally, after about 11 miles you reach the small town of **Annascaul**. Over a dozen pubs are available to let you stretch aching limbs and celebrate your achievements with a drink. Afterwards, a recommended place to lay your head is *Teac Seán (4 rooms | Main Street | tel. 066 9 15 70 01 | www.teacseain.com | Budget)*.

The stage goal for the third day is Dingle. However, before getting there, after a 14-mile hike and a 1115-ft ascent, enjoy the view of historic **Minard Castle**, which occupies a romantic location above little Kilmurry Bay. Carrying on through scattered villages finally takes you into lively **Dingle → p. 62** with its small port.

If all this has left you wanting more: the Dingle Way carries on west around **Slea Head**, a rough and lonely place full of old Gaelic remains: stone crosses, ring forts and ruins of Early Christian oratories. Heading north the Way carries on to Dunquin and back along the northern coast of the peninsula, past magnificent sandy beaches and below the Brendan mountain range.

Information and maps on the Dingle Way (including information on accommodation) is available from the tourist information office in Tralee *(Ashe Memorial Hall | Denny Street | tel. 066 7 12 12 88)*. For more in-depth information see *www.dingleway.net*.

Lonely farmstead on the Dingle Peninsula

the 7th century, making it older than the famous Gallarus Oratory! After 11 miles, the first day's stage has been completed once you reach the village of **Camp** (on the N 86), where you can also stay overnight *(5 rooms | Barnagh Bridge Country Guesthouse, Cappalough, Camp | tel. 066 7 13 01 45 | bbguest@eircom.net | Budget)*. Before that, you might want to sample a Guinness at *Ashe's* pub. If you've got energy left, head up to a ruined stone fort above Camp called **Cathair Chonroi** *(Caher Conree)*. The remains of the 110-metre-long wall, over four metres thick and three metres high, are worth the detour. The ascent takes

A CABIN CRUISER ON THE GRAND CANAL

From Dublin the Grand Canal leads via Robertstown and Tullamore to Shannon Harbour on the Shannon (77 miles). Our route follows the Canal east from Tullamore to Robertstown (12 miles), There, a branch of the Grand Canal leads south to Athy and meets the river Barrow, which you can navigate all the way to St Mullins (68 miles). Schedule at least a week for this easy-paced boat tour (there and back).

In the 19th century, the Grand Canal was a popular travel artery for up to 100,000 passengers a year, who took four days from Dublin to the Shannon, as the boats were drawn by horses. In 1960, the barge service was wound up. The typical **narrowboats** (narrower than those operating on the Shannon, at 230 miles the longest river in Ireland) may also be rented at the river Barrow *(Barrowline Cruisers | Vicarstown | tel. 057 8 62 60 60 | www.barrowline.ie)*. A four-bed boat costs around 1500 euros a week in July/August, at other times from 1100 euros. No boating licence is needed, as you are given a 30-minute induction before starting out. You potter along slowly through quiet nature, observing waterfowl, past overgrown stone bridges, historic sluices and old villages with inviting pubs.

Stock up on provisions in the whiskey town of **Tullamore**. The centre of the little town is formed by a broad street lined with shops and pubs. Sustenance can also be found at the Italian restaurant *Sirocco's (Patrick Street | tel. 057 9 35 28 39 | www.siroccos.net | Moderate)*, which does not just offer pizza and pasta, but also serves Irish dishes. In **Robertstown**, the goal of the next stage, the majestic Grand Canal Hotel dating back to the year 1801 has been renovated and serves traditional Irish fare in the *Old Style Restaurant (tel. 045 87 00 05 | Moderate)*. The same house shelters the *Canal Heritage Centre*. The former draught-horse path has been turned into a INSIDER TIP way perfect for a romantic stroll.

South of the town, a branch of the canal runs south, first to **Rathangan**, whose waters famously teem with a great variety of fish. For 150 years **Monasterevin** with its historic drawbridge housed a whiskey distillery, the ruins of which you

Anglers appreciate the peaceful nature on the green shores of the Grand Canal

can see from the canal. In the medieval market town of **Athy** the canal flows into the river Barrow. Now our route heads downriver, where 23 locks have to be overcome on the 40-mile stretch to St Mullins. In **Carlow** look out for the ruined Norman castle on the eastern shore. Via Muine Bheag, the river now carries on to Graiguenamanagh with **Duiske Abbey**, a restored Cistercian monastery dating back to 1207. The trip ends before you reach **St Mullins** at a lock, as the next section of the river to the estuary beyond New Ross is not suitable for light canal boats. If you've only booked your boat for one week you'll have to turn round now, in order to hand it back in good time: the boats only go at speeds of just over 6 mph,

and it's over 80 miles back to Tullamore. A description of all navigable canals and rivers in Ireland can be found in Jane Cumberlidge's The Inland Waterways of Ireland.

3 HISTORIC TOWNS OF THE SOUTH

From Cork, the N 22 leads west via Macroom and through the Derrynasaggart Mountains to Killarney, and from there on to Tralee. From Tralee take the N 21 northeast to reach Limerick. Going southeast, the route carries on to Tipperary, Cahir, Clonmel and Carrick-on-Suir. If you head for Youghal, you're on your way back to Cork. In the first in-

Popular theatre: join the fun at the Siamsa Tíre Theatre in Tralee

stance it's historic buildings that make this trip an enticing proposition, but also picturesque rivers and green mountainsides. Length: 280 miles. Duration: around four days.

From Cork → p. 46, the starting point of this driving tour, first head for the quiet market town of Macroom on the river Lee. The road winds its way past other small villages, often only hamlets really, through the Derrynasaggart Mountains to Killarney → p. 58 – for most travellers the finishing point of today's stage. In Tralee, with a population of 23,000 the largest town in County Kerry, it's worth taking in a visit to the Siamsa Tire Theatre (Town Park | tel. 066 712 30 55 | www. siamsatire), the island's best-known popular theatre, offering dance, music and a lot of song.

During the last week of August Tralee turns itself into one big open-air festival. The prettiest of all Irish girls – or girls of Irish descent – is elected the 'Rose of Tralee'; there are celebrations in the streets, music and horse betting. Beer consumption reaches its annual peak. If there are no free hotel beds because of this, you're better off driving on to Limerick → p. 67 or Tipperary. In Co. Tipperary, Cahir Castle, a national monument and the country's largest medieval fortification, is well worth visiting. Their audiovisual show is a good introduction to the life of the former castle dwellers. A hike along the river Suir is probably one of Ireland's best-kept secrets. On the river's shores you'll find the small town of Clonmel → p. 94, which exudes Irish charm with its greyhound racetrack and numerous pubs. Nature-lovers may choose to make a detour to Lismore and the valley of INSIDERTIP The Vee. The road (R 671) leads first over the river and then carries on in a southerly direction. On the way to Dungarvan turn right onto

a scenic route to Newcastle, Capoquin and finally Lismore. This pretty town is dominated by Lismore Castle (www. lismorecastle.com), whose oldest parts date back to the 12th century. While the castle is not open to the public, the splendid parks are accessible. Between magnolias, rhododendron and camellias discover modern sculptures, for instance by the English sculptor Anthony Gormley. Carry on now on the R 668 in the direction of Clogheen on a mainly bendy stretch, first across a raised bog and through romantic scenery of gurgling brooks and waterfalls, bog and moss, with a few sheep grazing. Gnarled old trees hang closely over narrow roads where you will meet few drivers. On the way, old-fashioned pubs beckon for a break.

Via numerous old stone bridges, past derelict quarry-stone cottages and lonely farmsteads, you'll again reach Clonmel. A good choice for accommodation is a historic coach station from the early 19th century by the name of Hearn's Hotel (25 rooms | 34/35 Parnell Street | tel. 052 2 16 11 | www.hearnshotel. ie | Moderate). The mid-range hotel is a meeting point for the town, also offering evening entertainment.

The next morning, on a hearty full Irish breakfast, head for Carrick-on-Suir → p. 93, where you might want to have a picnic in the gardens of the Elizabethan manor house of Ormond Castle, with a very pretty riverside location. Built in 1573 by the Earl of Ormond for the visit of Queen Elizabeth I, the mansion is connected with an older castle and possibly the birthplace of Anne Boleyn. Ormond Castle is only open in the summer. Via Youghal → p. 58 you finally reach the starting and finishing point of your round trip: Cork City.

SPORTS & ACTIVITIES

Golfing, horseback riding and fishing – Ireland has always combined rural life and country sports; these days there is a trend to activities such as hang-gliding and diving.

CANOE HIKING

Ireland's many lakes, rivers and canals are waiting to be paddled down, and even white-water rafting is possible. The most suitable rivers are the Liffey, Barrow, Shannon and Suir. Request the tourist board's *(www.discoverireland.com)* brochure on lakes and waterways. Information: *Irish Canoe Union, Sport HQ | 13 Joyce Way, Park West, Dublin 12 | tel. 01 6 25 11 05 | www.canoe.ie*

CYCLING

Bike tours are especially recommended in the scenic west and southwest. Rather than cycle paths, there are surfaced side roads with little traffic. Bikes can be hired nearly anywhere, e.g. at Shannon Airport by *Emerald Alpine (Roches Street, Limerick | tel. 061 41 69 83 | www.irelandrentabike.com)*. Bikes can be handed back at other places as well.

DIVING

Irish waters offer good visibility of up to 30 m. Flora (huge kelp forests) and fauna (schools of herring and seals) are varied, and the Gulf Stream ensures

A paradise for fishermen, golfers or horseback riders – only hardy folks jump into the cool Atlantic Ocean

bearable diving temperatures. The western side of the island has numerous wrecks, but the eastern coast too has interesting dive sites, accessible by boat. Information for scuba divers from: *Irish Underwater Council | 78A Patrick Street, Dun Laoghaire, Co. Dublin | tel. 01 2 84 46 01 | www.cft.ie.* A dive base with hire, service and accommodation is *Mevagh Dive Centre | Milford Rd., Carrigart, Co. Donegal | tel. 074 9 15 47 08 | www. mevaghdiving.com*

FISHING

Thousands of lakes, countless rivers and nearly 2000 miles of coastline – small wonder that there's hardly an Irish male who doesn't go fishing. Salmon populate the Atlantic rivers, trout live in most brooks and lakes *(game angling). Coarse angling* for pike, eel and other fish is also popular. Licences are available from angling shops. At the ports of Galway, Kinsale, Valentia Island and Youghal you can join deep-sea fishing expeditions, and several hotels offer fly-fishing packages *(www.flyfishing. com)*. Information: *Central Fisheries Board, Angling Division, Swords Business Campus, Swords | tel. 01 8 84 26 00.* For more information see: *www.cfb.ie.*

GOLFING

Ireland boasts 425 golf courses. Golfing is a popular pastime here, so green fees are low. A golfing guide and a list of golfing holiday operators is published by the Irish tourist board and under *www.dis-coverireland.ie/golf.* Small *pitch-and-putt* golf courses with fairways of 50–70 m can be found in nearly every village.

HANG GLIDING

The rolling hillsides, unspoilt bogs and the consistent Atlantic breeze offer ideal conditions for *hang gliding*. Before starting out get information on the regulations by consulting the *Irish Hang Gliding and Paragliding Association (www.ihpa.ie)*. One recommended operator is *Paragliding/Hang Gliding Centre | Kilmacanogue, Bray, Wicklow | tel. 01 8 31 45 51.*

HIKING

Many hiking trails have been laid out and signposted in scenic locations running across hills and along brooks, rivers and lakes. For information and descriptions of hiking trails in national parks see *www.npws.ie.* Dublin-based travellers without a car can now take advantage of the weekend Mountaineer bus (*www.dublinmountains.ie*) to get into the mountains – and back! Hikes in the coastal periphery of Dublin with committed guides, e.g. onto Muck Rock, on Lambay Island and on the cliffs above Howth, are run by *www.howthguidedtours. com.* Guided circular hikes are available through *www.walkinghikingireland.com* and *www.walktalkireland.com.* On *www. discoverireland.com* you will find descriptions of 14 circular hikes and the Walking & Cycling Holiday Guide.

There's plenty of water in Ireland: kayak lessons on Killary Fjord near Connemara

HOUSEBOATS / CABIN CRUISERS

Houseboats are available in all sizes (two to eight beds plus WC, shower, kitchen), with bikes and dinghy; motor yachts may also be hired. No need for a boating licence, as you are shown the ropes when you pick up the boat. A vessel sleeping four is no cheap pleasure – expect to pay 1500–2000 euros per week in high season. One rental operator is *Carrick Craft | Kinnego Marina, Oxford Island, Lurgan BT66 6NJ (Northern Ireland) | tel. 0044 28 38 34 49 93 | www.cruise-ireland.com;* pick-up and drop-off of the boats in Banagher, Carrick-on-Shannon or Tully Bay (one-way tours also available).

HORSE-DRAWN CARAVANS

The barrel-shaped horse-drawn wagons have space for up to four people. An operator near Dublin is *Clissmann Horse Caravans (Cronybyrne, Rathdrum, Co. Wicklow | tel. 0404 469 20 | www.cliss*

mann.com/wicklow). The tourist board has information on operators in counties Galway, Mayo and Wicklow. A caravan costs from 900 euros onwards (in July/Aug around 1200 euros) per week.

HORSERIDING

The Irish landscape is ideal for horseback riding. A renowned operator is *Horse Holiday Farm* in *Grange, County Sligo (tel. 071 9 16 61 52 | www.horseholidayfarm.net).* For information on 16 places to spend an equestrian holiday and other activities on horseback, see *www.ehi.ie.*

SAILING

Nearly 20,000 miles of coastline, 100 yachting clubs and 50 marinas surround the Emerald Isle. The ideal sailing area lies on the southern coast between Waterford and Kinsale. For more information contact the *Irish Sailing Association | 3 Park Road, Dun Laoghaire, Co. Dublin | tel. 01 2 80 02 39 | www.sailing.ie.*

SWIMMING & BEACHES

Ireland's beaches are amongst the cleanest in Europe, and dozens have already been awarded the Blue Flag (for water quality amongst other criteria). However, even on hot summer days the Atlantic is fairly cold (14–17 C°/57–61 F°). Dublin residents take the fast DART train to the resort of Bray 12 miles south; those not so keen on fish-and-chips vans and amusement arcades get off the train two stations further along in Killiney, with its natural pebble beach. Well known for sandy beaches against a dramatic coastal backdrop is Achill Island, and in summer, the resort of Waterville on the Iveragh Peninsula also offers tourist infrastructure.

TRAVEL WITH KIDS

Whether it's organised leisure time in a theme park or crabbing on their own at the seaside: far from the buzz of the city, children are welcomed with open arms in green Ireland.

IN AND AROUND DUBLIN

INSIDER TIP ▶ THE ARK
(U B4) (*ω b4*)

At the *Cultural Centre for Children*, toddlers are already encouraged to experiment with paints, wool and other materials to create objects of art that are then exhibited in the gallery. There are also inspiring theatre performances, as well as daily-changing shows and workshops. Reservations recommended. *11A Eustace Street, Temple Bar, Dublin 2 | Mon–Fri 10am–5pm | admission from 6 euros | www.ark.ie*

FRY MODEL RAILWAY (131 E3) (*ω K11*)

A castle for the parents and a miniature train for children: hand-made models, many manufactured by a railway engineer in the 1920s and 1930s, run on 250 square metres. *Malahide Castle Demesne Malahide, Co. Dublin | Tue–Sat 10am–1pm, Sun 1–5pm | admission adults 6, children 4, families 15 euros | www.malahidecastle.com*

INSIDER TIP ▶ GREENAN FARM MUSEUMS & MAZE
(131 F 5–6) (*ω K12*)

A pleasant day of learning and fun, outside when the sun is out, inside

Child-friendly Ireland: the Emerald Isle has the youngest population in Europe – families everywhere can expect a sincere welcome

when it's raining, on a farm with many animals, plus a farmhouse museum in a 16th-century building. Even for adults, the maze is difficult to navigate. Crafts as well as fresh *scones* and pastries are available from the tearoom. *Ballinanty near Greenan, Rathdrum, Co. Wicklow | May/June Tue–Sun 10am–6pm, July/Aug daily 10am–6pm, Sept Sun 10am–6pm | admission adults 8, children 6, families 24 euros | www.greenanmaze.com*

IMAGINOSITY (131 E4) (*K11*)
In this interactive facility in the Dublin suburb of Sandyford there are models and installations, allowing children up to nine years of age to give free rein to their imagination and creativity: building, painting, climbing and acting. *The Plaza, Beacon South Quarter Sandyford | LUAS tram to Stillorgan, buses 114/75/46B and 11A to Blackthorn Road | Mon 1.30–5.30pm, Tue–Fri 9.30am–5.30pm, Sat/Sun 10am–6pm | admission adults and children 8 euros | www.imaginosity.ie*

THE SOUTH

AQUA DOME (132 C3) (*C15*)

Large waterworld leisure complex with various slides, waves, pools and boats; also minigolf and different games. *Wet, Wild & Wonderful | Tralee, Co. Kerry | Dan Spring Road (at the Dingle Road Junction in the south of town on the River Lee) | Mon–Fri 10am–10pm, Sat/Sun 11am–8pm | admission adults 15, children 12 euros | www.aquadome.ie*

VALENTIA HARBOUR TOURS (132 A–B4) (*A–B16*)

A special amphibian vehicle – a large boat on three wheels – can take up to 48 passengers on a fun harbour tour between Valentia Island and the mainland. On the trip you'll pass ruined ring forts, monastic settlements and the port of Knightstown, while seals loll about on small rocky islets. *Valentia Harbour Tours | Cahersiveen, Ring of Kerry | duration of the trip 1.5 hrs | adults 16, children 10 euros | tel. 087 0 52 75 62 | www.valentia harbourtours.com*

FOTA WILDLIFE PARK (134 A6) (*F 16*)

The wildlife park shelters some 90 kinds of animals in outdoor enclosures, amongst them giraffes and cheetahs. Children enjoy the daily feeding session in the early morning and late afternoon. *Fota Island, at Carrigtwohill (near Cork) | Mon–Sat 10am–6pm, Sun 11am–6pm | admission adults 13.50, children 9, families 44 euros | www.fota wildlife.ie*

INSIDER TIP SEAFARI (132 C4) (*C16*)

Pack a warm jacket, this is the sea: the boat trip to see seals on the Kenmare River and in Kenmare Bay takes two hours. Over 150 animals live off the coast here, and you're guaranteed to see some during this tour. *Henry Street Pier Kenmare | April–Oct, tours are dependent on the tides | trip per person 22 euros per person, families 60 euros | tel. 064 6 64 20 59 | www.seafariireland. com*

Sometimes happiness is a small board: boys surfing in Kilkee

THE WEST COAST

ATLANTAQUARIA (128 C4) (*m D11*)
Fish and other sea creatures inhabit 2000 square metres of a natural-looking universe. The reconstructed lighthouse houses a café, and in the submarine visitors can experience a simulated diving expedition. *National Aquarium | The Promenade Salthill, Galway | daily 9am–5pm (Oct–Feb closed Mon/Tue) | admission 10.25, children 6.25 euros | www.national aquarium.ie*

DOLPHINWATCH (132 C1) (*m C14*)
The Shannon estuary shelters a colony of dolphins, which can be visited on two-hour boat tours. *Kilcredaun near Carrigaholt, Co. Clare (37 mi west of Ennis) | tours April–Sept | ticket adults 24, children 12 euros | tel. 065 9 05 81 56 | www. dolphinwatch.ie*

LAHINCH SEAWORLD & LEISURE CENTRE (128 C5) (*m C13*)
A mix of play and climbing area, swimming pool and splash pool, jacuzzi, sauna and aquarium. Your entertainment is assured for the entire day. *The Promenade Lahinch, Co. Clare | May–Sept daily 10am–6pm, Oct–April 10am–5pm | admission adults 14, children 10 euros | www.lahinchseaworld.com*

LEISURE LAND (128 C4) (*m D11*)
This leisure complex offers a swimming pool, a 65-metre slide, a pirate ship and (Easter–Sept) a fun fair. *The Promenade Salthill, Galway | Mon–Fri 7am–10.30pm, Sat/Sun 9am–8pm | admission adults 10, children 8 euros | www.leisureland.ie*

THE MIDLANDS

FETHARD FOLK, FARM AND TRANSPORT MUSEUM (134 C3) (*m G14*)
City kids can learn a lot about rural life here: the old railway station at the edge of Fethard shows 1200 objects, amongst them many historic means of transportation and vehicles such as carriages and prams. There's a play area for children too. *Cashel Road (R 692) Fethard, Co. Tipperary | Sun 11am–5pm | admission farm area 2 euros, museum 1.50 euros | www. fethard.com*

PARSONS GREEN PARK AND PET FARM (134 B4) (*m F15*)
Here children and adults may visit riverside gardens, a farm museum and an animal enclosure, or sweat in the Viking sauna. Sporty types can go pony-riding, take a boat tour on the river, or try a round of tennis, basketball or crazy golf with many unusual obstacles. If you want to stay longer, stay on the campsite or rent an apartment. *Clogheen, Co. Tipperary | April–Sept daily 10am–8pm | admission adults 4, children 3, families 15 euros | www.clogheen.com*

FESTIVALS & EVENTS

Summer on the Emerald Isle is accompanied by events and festivals. Some of them – such as the Cork Jazz Festival – are internationally known. The *fleadh* festivals are exclusively dedicated to traditional music – dancing allowed!

HOLIDAYS

1 Jan *New Year;* **17 March** *St Patrick's Day (national holiday);* **Easter Monday; 1st Monday in May** *May Day;* **1st Monday in June** *Bank Holiday;* **1st Monday in Aug** *Bank Holiday;* **last Monday in Oct** *Bank Holiday;* **25 Dec** *Christmas;* **26 Dec** *St Stephen's Day*

FESTIVALS

Every village has its own festival, and there's usually some kind of celebration going on somewhere in Ireland. Any combination of the following elements is usually involved: music, dance, horses, theatre, agriculture, sports, boats, racing, food and drink. Contact the Irish tourist board for an exhaustive *Calendar of Festivals & Events.*

JANUARY

▶ INSIDER TIP *Temple Bar Traditional Festival of Irish Music:* a five-day session in late January for folk musicians on the fiddle, bodhrán and banjo. *www.templebartrad.com*

MARCH

▶ ★ ● *St Patrick's Festival, mid-March:* around the national holiday of St Patrick's Day, all of Dublin parties for five days on the streets, with parades, dance, acrobatics and entertainment. *www.stpatricksfestival.ie*

JUNE

▶ *Bloomsday*, 16 June: one day in the life of Leopold Bloom in 1904, described in vast detail by James Joyce in his monumental novel Ulysses. That fateful day is repeated for his followers in lectures, walks and visits to the pub. *Dublin | www.jamesjoyce.ie*

JULY

▶ *Galway Arts Festival*, second half of the month: two weeks of arts and theatre, dance and music, comedy, literature and film. *Tel. 091 50 97 00 | www.galwayartsfestival.ie*

AUGUST

▶ *Kilkenny Arts Festival*, ten days in mid-August: arts and music festival ranging

Music and dancing form the main ingredients of Irish celebrations – especially the highlight of the calendar: St Patrick's Day, the national holiday

from cathedral concerts to street theatre. *Tel. 056 775 2175 | www.kilkennyarts.ie*

▶ ● **INSIDER TIP** *Fleadh Cheoil na hEireann*, second half of the month: three days of Irish folk music – in pubs, hotels and schools, even on the street. Every year the fleadh (pronounced 'flaa' as in the noise sheep make) takes place in a different town. *www.comhaltas.com*

▶ *Dublin Horse Show*, for five days in August horses take centre stage: dressage and jumping competitions, horse shows and a major horse fair. *www.dublin horseshow.com*

▶ *Puck Fair*, mid-month: authentic rural fair with lots of music, cattle and horse fair and 100,000 visitors. The action revolves around a male goat, the puck. *Tel. 066 976 23 66 | Killorglin, Kerry | www. puckfair.ie*

▶ *Rose of Tralee International Festival*, five days in August: a beauty contest for young Irish women (or women of Irish descent) with plenty of open-air concerts. *Tel. 066 712 13 22 | Tralee | www.roseoftralee.ie*

SEPTEMBER

▶ *Galway Oyster Festival:* four-day gourmet festival in late September featuring fresh fish, lots of Guinness and oysters. *www.galwayoysterfest.com*

▶ *Dublin Theatre Festival* end of Sept–mid Oct: classic plays plus experimental theatre. *www.dublintheatrefestival.com*

OCTOBER

▶ *Kinsale Gourmet Festival*, three days of culinary events in Kinsale. *www.kinsale restaurants.com*

▶ *Guinness Jazz Festival*, four days in late Oct in Cork: for decades a near-legendary event attracting jazz greats from all over the world, with sessions and rhythms at nearly every street corner. *www.cork jazzfestival.com*

▶ *Wexford Festival Opera*, second half of Oct: for 60 years, the small town has been showing forgotten and little-known operas. *Wexford | www.wexfordopera. com*

LINKS, BLOGS, APPS & MORE

LINKS

▶ www.heritageireland.ie Everything you need to know about the country's cultural history and historic buildings.

▶ www.discoverireland.ie/festivals The website keeps you up to date on the countless events and festivals taking place on the island, the Festival of the Erne in Belturbet for instance, that you'd have been unlikely to hear about otherwise

▶ www.spottedbylocals.com These kind people share their Dublin gems with the online community

▶ www.ireland-fun-facts.com Readable collection of curiosities, plus unusual travel ideas

▶ www.thephoenix.ie The homepage of the Irish satirical magazine inspired by Private Eye allows you to view an entire recent edition, pulling the rug from under political, social and assorted posturing

▶ www.mythicalireland.com The website reveals the secret and mythical side of the Emerald Isle: the holy stones and ritual sites of the megalithic period

APPS

▶ Around Me At a click, this programme by Tweakersoft reveals what's around you: cafés, restaurants, cinemas, theatre, hotels etc., with city map and distances

▶ Dublin Bus Type in your destination or bus route to receive the departure times (including the last bus!) on your iPhone

▶ Visit Dublin App This useful app for iPhone and Android uses 'camera view' and 'guide me' to lead you to sights, hotels and restaurants. You can even point it at a historic building you're passing and it'll tell you what you're looking at

▶ Ireland's Blue Book This free app offers geographical guides to classy manor houses, castles and country estates

Regardless of whether you are still preparing your trip or already in Ireland: these addresses will provide you with more information, videos and Networksss to make your holiday even more enjoyable

BLOGS

▶ www.dublinblog.ie A community of dedicated Dubliners blogging about life in the Irish capital

VIDEOS & PODCASTS

▶ video.ireland.com Varied impressions from the island: from sightings of humpback whales to a performance by the Dublin Gospel Choir

▶ http://vodpod.com/tag/ireland Website featuring lots of videos – from Giant's Causeway to Kilkenny Castle

▶ http://www.discoverireland.com/gb/ The locals show off their island for the Irish tourist board: landscapes and myths, outdoor activities, music and pretty places

▶ http://www.thisisirishfilm.ie/ The Irish Film Board's media hub is a great showcase of fillums

▶ www.visitdublin.com/iwalks Download audioguides and walks in Dublin as podcasts

NETWORKS

▶ www.couchsurfing.org A free hospitality site with thousands of active Couch-surfers around the whole island, looking for cultural exchange with like-minded people. Dublin is a popular destination; make sure you put some work into your profile!

▶ twitter.com/Ireland This community is mainly interested in the arts and culture

▶ twitter.com/dubcitycouncil Up-to-date information from the Irish capital

▶ http://de-de.facebook.com/liveireland Ireland's facebook friends uphold Irish heritage and are a great fan of Dublin's chief rockers U2

TRAVEL TIPS

ACCOMMODATION

Sadly, the quality of accommodation in Ireland often doesn't quite correlate with the price. The tourist board will send lists of inspected bed & breakfast places, as well as holiday cottages and apartments. On the face of it, the cheapest choice after hostels are B & Bs, though once you factor in having to dine out, you'll be paying much more than for a week's self-catering. In towns, the price per person ranges between 40 and 55 euros, depending on the level of comfort: *www.bandbireland.com*.

In high season, holiday apartments cost from 300 euros upwards, holiday cottages from 600 euros per week. Information and booking though: *Irish Cottage Holiday Homes, Bracken Court, Bracken Road, Sandyford, Dublin 18 | tel. 01 2 05 27 77 | www.irishcottageholidays.com*.

The websites *www.hiddenhr.com* and *www.irelands-blue-book.ie* lead you to small but beautiful accommodation choices. For a list of exclusive hotels housed in former castles and manor houses contact *Ireland's Blue Book (7/8 Mountain Street Crescent, Dublin 2 | tel. 01 6 76 99 14 | www.irelandsbluebook.com)* or see *www.manorhousehotels.com* (all expensive). A selection of country hotels is available at *www.irishcountryhotels.com*. A search engine for hotels (incl. special offers) is *www.hotelsireland.com*.

For holidays on a farm: *Irish Farmhouse Holidays | 2 Michael Street, Limerick | tel. 061 40 07 00 | www.irishfarmholidays.com*. Some 20 farms offer working holidays on farms. Travellers interested in *WWOOF (Willing Worker on Organic Farms)* can approach member farmers direct: *www.irishorganic.ie*. Unusual accommodation such as a lighthouse or a castle can be booked through *The Irish Landmark Trust (25 Eustace Street, Dublin 2 | tel. 01 6 70 47 33 | www.irishlandmark.com)*.

RESPONSIBLE TRAVEL

It doesn't take a lot to be environmentally friendly whilst travelling. Don't just think about your carbon footprint whilst flying to and from your holiday destination but also about how you can protect nature and culture abroad. As a tourist it is especially important to respect nature, look out for local products, cycle instead of driving, save water and much more. If you would like to find out more about eco-tourism please visit: *www.ecotourism.org*

ARRIVAL

Ferries routes from Britain are Holyhead-Dun Laoghaire and Liverpool-Dublin, *(www.poferries.com)*, Fishguard to Rosslare and Stranraer to Belfast *(www.stenaline.co.uk)*; the Swansea to Cork route *(www.fastnetonline.com)* is again in doubt, but there's a new Liverpool to Belfast route *(www.stenaline.co.uk)*. Look for special offers on fare-comparing sites such as *www.ferriestoireland.net* or *www.cheapferry.co.uk*.

The famous budget carrier Ryanair *(www.ryanair.com)* flies from London to Dublin and Kerry. Air France has services from New York to Dublin via Paris.

From arrival to weather

From the start to the end of the holiday: useful addresses and information for your Ireland trip

The state carrier Aer Lingus *(www.aerlingus.com)* has turned itself into a low-cost airline, offering direct flights from New York to Dublin and Shannon (an airport handy for the west, but with decreasing traffic these days) and from Boston, Chicago and Orlando to Dublin. Connections within Ireland are offered by Aer Arann *(www.aerarann.com)*.

From Dublin airport to the city centre, the scheduled buses no. 41, 16 A and 46 X (2.20 euros) take up to 45 min., with a lot of stops, express buses no. 747 and no. 748 (6 euros, Airlink) approx. 20–30 min.; at night, the buses 33 N and 41 N can take you into the city centre and to the railway stations (4 euros). A taxi from the airport to the centre costs around 25 euros, approx. 15–25 min. To take advantage of cheap flights at unsociable hours, the two airport hotels *(www.clarionhoteldublinairport.com, www.radissonblu.ie/hotel-dublinairport)* do brisk business; the Clarion has the nicer food and ambience.

BANKS & CREDIT CARDS

Opening times of the banks: *Mon–Fri 10am–12.30pm, 1.30–3pm or 5pm.* Cashpoints of Allied Irish Bank (AIB) or Bank of Ireland are available in towns and most larger villages; they take debit and credit cards. Credit cards are widely accepted.

CAMPING

Ireland has more than 200 officially recognised campsites. Request the Caravan & Camping Parks brochure from the Irish tourist board *(www.discoverireland.com)*, who can also provide the Caravan, Camping & Motorhome Guide. Small camper vans, also called *bunk campers* here, as they feature two or four bunk beds, have no bathroom, shower or WC, but do have a kitchenette and fridge. For rental, contact *Bunk Campers (in summer: 90 euros per day with two, 120 euros with four beds | www.bunkcampers.com).*

CAR HIRE

To hire a car you have to be at least 21, for higher categories even 23 or 25. A

CURRENCY CONVERTER

£	€	€	£
1	1.10	1	0.90
3	3.30	3	2.70
5	5.50	5	4.50
13	14.30	13	11.70
40	44	40	36
75	82.50	75	67.50
120	132	120	108
250	275	250	225
500	550	500	450

$	€	€	$
1	0.70	1	1.40
3	2.10	3	4.20
5	3.50	5	7
13	9.10	13	18.20
40	28	40	56
75	52.50	75	105
120	84	120	168
250	175	250	350
500	350	500	700

For current exchange rates see www.xe.com

national driving licence in English is sufficient. A car costs from 35 euros per day, more if you'll be going to Northern Ireland. To avoid high charges at pick-up (e.g. a block of 1200 euros on your credit card if full insurance is not chosen), book your car (with fully comprehensive insurance) before you travel. At least the rental car companies take care of the M50 toll, which is read automatically. A new tunnel makes for easier access to the Docklands area, but costs 10 euros on weekdays, 3 euros at weekends.

CLIMATE, WHEN TO GO

In winter temperatures hardly ever fall below 0 °C /°F 32 – though recent winters have been exceptionally harsh, with widespread snow and ice. Summer temperatures then rarely inch over the 25 °C / 77 F° mark. Rain is always on the cards, particularly in the west. May and June are the sunniest months, while July and August are the high season for tourism.

CONSULATES & EMBASSIES

UK EMBASSY
29 Merrion Road | Ballsbridge | Dublin 4 | tel. 01 2 50 37 00 | http://britishembassy inireland.fco.gov.uk

US EMBASSY
42 Elgin Road | Ballsbridge | Dublin 4 | tel. 01 6 68 87 77 | http://dublin.usembassy. gov

CUSTOMS

Within the European Union, EU citizens over 17 may freely import and export goods for personal use, e.g. 800 cigarettes, 90 litres of wine and 10 litres of spirits. North American citizens are subject to much lower allowances, in-cluding only 200 cigarettes and 1 litre of spirits. Personal defence sprays etc. are illegal in Ireland. For accessibly presented information, see *www.citizens information.ie*

DRIVING

Ireland, like the UK, drives on the left. Top speed in built-up areas is 50 km/h, on country roads 100 km/h. Regional country roads are often quite narrow; accidents are more likely to occur on those – and in this small society are reported nationally. The drink-driving limit is at 0.8. While lowering it to 0.5 is being discussed, it is controversial, as in rural areas, pubs function as social centres. In Ireland , EU citizens only need their national or European licence. North American licences are accepted too. Fines (e. g. for drink-driving, speeding, parking offences) are very high, and drink-driving over the limit will set you back at least 1270 euros. The network of motorways In Ireland has improved beyond recognition.

DISCOUNTS FOR TOURISTS

A free *Discount Pass* valid for 90 sights and cultural institutions may be downloaded and printed from the *www. cultureheritageireland.com* site. The *Ireland's Visitor Attractions Guide*, available online *(6.99 euros | www.heritageisland. com)*, offers a *Discount Pass* with discounted access (often 2 for 1) to 89 sights. For 21 euros, the *Heritage Card (www. heritageireland.ie)* gives you access to 96 heritage sites. To take advantage of the free *Ireland vouchers* giving discounts (often 2-for-1) at 76 sights and numerous activities, contact the tourist board.

ELECTRICITY

Voltage: 220 volts; British appliances work without adapters; North Americans need to bring a US two-to-three pin adapter.

EMERGENCY

Nationwide emergency number for police, fire service or mountain/coastal rescue: 999 or 112

HEALTH

Chemists or pharmacies are often attached to a drugstore. In cities, there is always an emergency pharmacy provision; information on the location of the relevant pharmacy is posted in the window of drugstores. British citizens should bring their EHIC (European Health Insurance Card) or a replacement certificate, which entitles you to free emergency treatment at hospitals, GPs' surgeries and dentists.

HOSTELS

Of the 26 state-run youth hostels, grouped together in the *Irish Youth Hostel Association – An Oige*, half are open all year round. There is no age limit. An overnight stay costs between 15 and 30 euros. For a list, contact the *Irish Youth Hostel Association (61 Mountjoy Street, Dublin 7 | tel. 01 8 30 45 55 | www.anoige.ie).*
There are also about 80 independent hostels (from 12 eurohoo.des) listed in the *Guide to Independent Holiday Hostels,* available from *Independent Hostels.* Book online at *www.hostels-ireland.com*

IMMIGRATION

UK citizens need a valid passport or UK/ Irish driving licence – the latter is only sufficient if you were born in the UK or Ireland before 1983. North American citizens require a passport but no visa for a holiday.

INFORMATION

IRELAND INFORMATION
UK: *103 Wigmore St | London W1U 1QS | tel. 0207 518 0800 | www.discoverireland. com/gb*
US: *345 Park Avenue | 17th Floor / New York, NY 10154, USA | tel. 0212 418 0800 | www.discoverireland.com/us*
Alongside the official tourist board website *www.discoverireland.com,* another good source of information before starting out is *http://www.ceolas.org/IrishNet*, linking the Irish and Irish-interest sites all over the world.

LANGUAGE

In the west, northwest and on the islands you'll hear a smattering of Irish, the language of the ancient Celts, alongside English. Road signs are bilingual.

BUDGETING

Guinness	From 4 euros for a pint
Cream tea	From 4.50 euros for scones and tea
Coffee	3–3.50 euros for a latte
Bus ticket	11.70 euros for a single from Dublin to Cork
Petrol	Approx. 1.50 euros for a litre of plus unleaded
Lunch	9–12 euros for a pub lunch

Living like the Irish: rent a cottage in the northwest of Ireland

PRICES

While the recession has lead to a decline in business in Ireland too, and thus to slightly lower prices, living costs remain very high on the island. Dublin in particular is expensive – if you want to sit down to eat. Even a simple pizza or pasta dish can set you back nearly 20 euros, a little soup with bread in a restaurant around 10 euros. Within Europe, prices for groceries are only higher in Denmark. Apart from hostels, accommodation is expensive too compared to other European countries. It's worth planning ahead!

PUBLIC TRANSPORT

Bus Éireann (www.buseireann.ie) offers an *Open Road Pass* (e. g. 3 out of 6 days 54 euros; 4 out of 8 days 69 euros; 5 out of 10 days 84 euros). Dublin and other large towns have a good public transport system; *Dublin Area Rapid Transport (DART)* runs along the coast. The *Iarnród Éireann (www.irishrail.ie)* network covers all counties but Donegal and offers the *Irish Explorer Bus & Rail Ticke*t (8 out of 15 consecutive days cost 245 euros).

Senior citizens can even take advantage of a free ride: the *Golden Trekker Card* allows travellers from 66 and up to travel by Irish Rail for four consecutive days, three times a year, .i.e. you can use it three times on a two-week trip, but it has to be requested at least three days before arrival *(www.discoverireland.com/goldentrekker).*

PHONE & MOBILE PHONE

The country code for Ireland is: *00353*, UK: *0044*, USA/Canada *001*. Card phones are widespread; phone cards for 10, 15 or 20 euros are available from the post office.

Mobile/cells: using an Irish prepaid SIM card avoids paying for incoming calls. Vodafone has the best coverage, but good-value SIM cards are also available from O2 *(www.o2.ie)* and Meteor *(www.meteor.ie)* from 15 euros. Texting is always the cheapest option. Listening to messages on your mailbox is an expensive luxury: turn it off before you travel, as this can only be done in the country of origin! Irish mobiles/cells operate on GSM standard.

TIME

Ireland runs on GMT Western European time, like the UK.

TIPPING

Taxi fares should be rounded up; in restaurants a tip of around 10 per cent (if not already on the bill) is adequate. Hotel maids usually get 1 euro per day. Petrol bills at serviced petrol stations should be rounded up too.

WEIGHTS & MEASURES

Despite Ireland's switch to the decimal system, you'll often find the imperial weight and measures still used:

1 foot (12 inches):	30.5 cm
1 gallon (8 pints):	4.48 l
1 inch:	2.54 cm
1 mile:	1.609 km
1 pint:	0.56 l
1 pound:	453 g
1 yard (3 feet):	91.4 cm

WIFI

Many shopping malls, restaurants, coffeeshops and hotels offer wireless internet access. Internet cafés are available in all larger towns: *www.cybercafes.com*. You can also try the library.

WEATHER IN DUBLIN

	Jan	Feb	March	April	May	June	July	Aug	Sept	Oct	Nov	Dec
Daytime temperatures in °C/°F	8/46	8/46	10/50	12/54	15/59	18/64	20/68	19/66	17/63	14/57	10/50	8/46
Nighttime temperatures in °C/°F	2/36	2/36	2/36	3/37	6/43	9/48	11/52	10/50	9/48	6/43	3/37	2/36
Sunshine hours/day	2	3	4	6	7	7	6	5	4	3	2	2
Precipitation days/month	13	11	10	11	11	11	13	13	12	12	12	13
Water temperature in °C/°F	9/48	8/46	7/45	8/46	9/48	11/52	13/55	14/57	14/57	13/55	12/54	10/50

NOTES

FOR YOUR NEXT HOLIDAY ...

MARCO POLO TRAVEL GUIDES

ALGARVE
AMSTERDAM
BARCELONA
BERLIN
BUDAPEST
CORFU
DUBROVNIK & DAL-
  MATIAN COAST
DUBAI
EDINBURGH
FINLAND
FLORENCE
FLORIDA
FRENCH RIVIERA
  NICE, CANNES &
  MONACO

IRELAND
KOS
LAKE GARDA
LANZAROTE
LONDON
MADEIRA
  PORTO SANTO
MALLORCA
MALTA
  GOZO
NEW YORK

NORWAY
PARIS
RHODES
ROME
SAN FRANCISCO
STOCKHOLM
THAILAND
VENICE

MARCO POLO
With ROAD ATLAS & PULL-OUT MAP
LAKE GARDA
E BALDO WITH MOUNTAIN BIKE
to Malcesine takes bikes too
SES" IN SALÒ
ate "baceti"
Travel with
Insider
Tips

MARCO POLO
With STREET ATLAS & PULL-OUT MAP
NEW YORK
OWS, WILD FLOWERS AND SKYSCRAPERS
chic: the High Line in Chelsea
SAIL ON CLOUD NINE
top bar at 230 Fifth Street
Travel with
Insider
Tips

MARCO POLO
With ROAD ATLAS & PULL-OUT MAP
FRENCH RIVIERA
NICE, CANNES & MONACO
SPECTACULAR GRAND CANYON DU VERDON
Breath-taking scenery that takes some beating
SNIFFING THE AIR
The perfume manufacturers of Grasse
Travel with
Insider
Tips
www.marcopolouk.com

MARCO POLO
With ROAD ATLAS & PULL-OUT MAP
ALLORCA
AN FLAIR IN THE MEDITERRANEAN
Mallorca's most beautiful beach
E IN" CROWD MEET
onia in Deià
Travel with
Insider
Tips

MARCO POLO
With STREET ATLAS & PULL-OUT MAP
BERLIN
A STUNNING ISLAND JUST FOR ART
Showcasing treasures from around the world
STAY COOL AT NIGHT
scene sets the trend
Travel with
Insider
Tips

- PACKED WITH INSIDER TIPS
- BEST WALKS AND TOURS
- FULL-COLOUR PULL-OUT MAP
  AND STREET ATLAS

ROAD ATLAS

The green line ▬▬ indicates the Trips & tours (p. 96–101)
The blue line ▬▬ indicates the Perfect route (p. 30–31)

All tours are also marked on the pull-out map

Photo: Portnablagh near Donegal

Exploring Ireland

The map on the back cover shows how the area
has been sub-divided

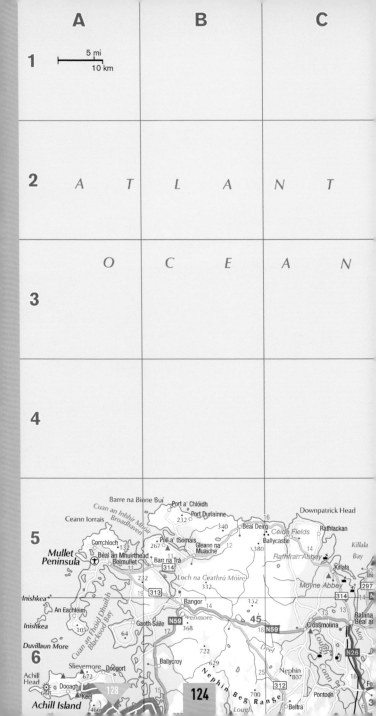

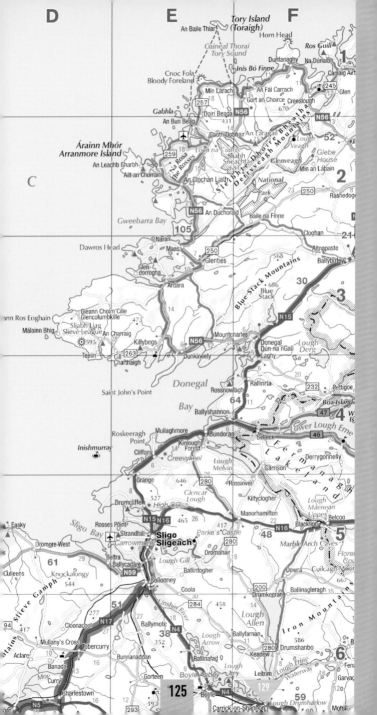

Tory Island
(Toraigh)
An Baile Thiar
Cainéal Thoraí
Tory Sound
Horn Head
Ros Guill

1

Inis Bó Finne
Cnoc Fola
Bloody Foreland
Gabhla
An Bun Beag
Doiri Beaga
N56
Gaoth Dobhair
An Earagail Bhéarbha
Loch na Cuinge
Sliabh
Sneachta
Áilt an Chorráin
An Clochán Liath
An Duchoraid
Baile na Finne
Dunfanaghy
Na Dúnaibh
Carraig Airt
Glen
245
N56
Min Lárach
An Fál Carrach
Gort an Choirce
Creeslough
670
257
259
Árainn Mhór
Arranmore Island
An Leadhb Gharbh
Na Rosa
the Rosses
Derryveagh Mountains
Glenveagh
Glebe
House
Min an Lábáin
National
Park
250
Rashedoge

52

Lough
Veagh

2

Gweebarra Bay
105
Dawros Head
Naran
Maas
250
Glenties
568
Altnapaste
Ballybofey
Glen-
dorragha
Ardara
Blue Stack Mountains
Blue
Stack
686
N15

30

3

Gleann Choilm Cille
Glencolumbkille
Sliabh Liag
Slieve League
Málainn Bhig
Teelin
Cill
Charthaigh
263
Killybegs
Dunkineely
N56
Mountcharles
Donegal
Dún na nGall
Laghy
Lough
Derg
Pettigoe
Ros Eoghain
473
595
An Charraig

Saint John's Point
Donegal
Bay
Rossnowlagh
Rahinta
Ballyshannon
64
Bundoran
232
Boa Island
47
46
Lower Lough Erne
Derrygonnelly

4

W

Roskeeragh
Point
Inishmurray
Muilaghmore
Kinlough
Forest
Cliffony
Creevykeel
Lough
Melvin
Rossinver
Garrison
Belleek
Fermanagh
Lakeland
Lough
Macnean
Upper
Belcoo

Grange
Drumcliff
High Cross
527
646
Glencar
Lough
280
Kiltyclogher
Manorhamilton
Blacklion
Easky
Dromore West
Culleens
61
Rosses Point
Strandhill
Carrowmore
N15 N16
Sligo
Sligeach
465
417
Parke's Castle
22
N16
Marble Arch Caves
Florence
Cou

5

Sligo Bay
Knockalongy
544
Beltra
Ballycadrea
N59
Collooney
Coola
284
458
Lough Gill
Dromahair
Ballintogher
200
Drumkeeran
Dowra
Cuilcagh Moun
667

48

Iron Mountains

94
417
Mullany's Cross
Aclare
Banada
Moy
Curry
Cloonacool
N17
Tobercurry
Bunnanaddan
277
27
352
Ballymote
N4
Gorteen
Ballinafad
Boyle Abbey
Lough
Arrow
Ballyfarnan
Lough
Key
Keadew
280
Drumshanbo
586
Leitrim
Lough Allen
Iron Mountain
Lough Fring
Waterway
Garvag
Fena

6

Charlestown
16
N5
293
Boyle
N4
Carrick-on-Shannon
Lough Drumharlow
Mohill

59

125
129

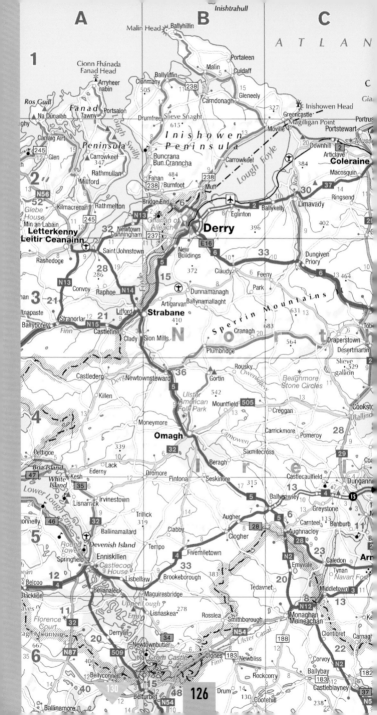

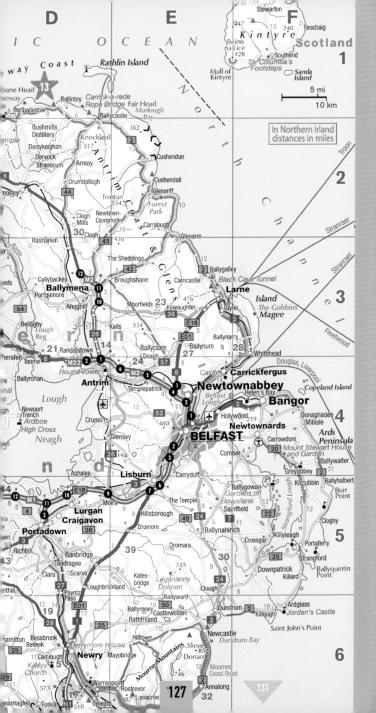

1

Stewarton

447 10 240 Feochaig

Kintyre

Scotland

Beinn
na Lice 428

Mull of
Kintyre

St Columba's
Footsteps

*Sanda
Island*

IC OCEAN

eway Coast

Rathlin Island

bane Head

*Carrick-a-rede
Rope Bridge* Fair Head

Ballintoy Murlough
Bay

Portballintrae Ballycastle

13

Bushmills
Distillery

Derrykeighan

Dervock Stranocum

Knocklayd
517 382

Antrim Coast

Cushendun

In Northern Irland
distances in miles

2

5 mi

10 km

North

Armoy

Drumdallagh

44

Clogh
Mills

30 Clogh

Rasharkin

Trostan
554

Newtown-
Crommelin

Cushendall

Glenariff
Forest
Park

Carnlough

10

Glenarm

Channel

Stranraer

Stranraer

Coast

54

Bellaghy
Lough
Beg

Cullybackey
Portglenore

Ballymena

Ahoghill

Randalstown

Toome

Ballyronan

e r n

21

12 M2

11

10

Keils

26

354

43 436

The Sheddings

Broughshane

Moorfields 23

Kilwaughter

Kells

Ballyclare

14 Doagh

42

Carncastle

2 Ballygalley

Black Cave Tunnel

Glens

Larne

476 *Island*

The Gobbins

Magee

Glynn

E18

E01 Bailynure

3

2

Ballynarry

Fleetwood

57 27

28

Whitehead

Douglas, Liverpool

6 M22

2

Round Tower

Antrim

Lough

Newport
Trench
Ardboe
High Cross

Neagh

Antrim

Templepatrick

52

480

Crumlin

Glenavy

2

24

M2 5

8

Castle

4

Carrickfergus

Newtownabbey

1 2

Belfast
Lough 8

Helen's Bay

Bangor

Copeland Island

Donaghadee
Millisle

**Ards
Peninsula**

Holywood 19

Carrowdore

20 Mount Stewart House
and Garden

Ballywalter

12

4

BELFAST

Newtownards

26

194

Aghalee

Lisburn

3

7 6

Moira

E18

10

12 M1

11

4

2

Portadown

Richhill

Banbridge

Clara

Tandragee
Scarva

27

Loughbrickland

19 14

28

E01

1

25

Poyntz
Pass

Ballyroney
Castlewellan
Rathfriland

Bessbrook
Belleek

11 Camlough
Killévy
Church

Newry

Mayobridge

Warrenpoint

Rostrevor
Lisnacree

577

Omeath

N1 510

Craigavon

Lurgan

26

9

Dromore

39

535

Katesbridge

*Légananny
Dolmen*

Ballyward

Clough

Hilltown

Dromara

Comber

Carryduff

The Temple

Ballygowan
Gardens of
Rowallane
Saintfield

49 24

Ballynahinch

30

Crossgar

Strangford Lough

Greyabbey

2 21

Ballyhalbert

Kircubbin

22

Burr
Point

12

Cloghy

Killyleagh

25

Downpatrick

Strangford

Killard

Portaferry

Ballyquintin
Point

5

24

Dundrum

Killough

2

Newcastle
Dundrum Bay

Slieve
852
Donard

Mourne Mountains

746 132

*Mournes
Coast Road*

Mayobridge

2

Annalong

32

Ardglass
Jordan's Castle

Saint John's Point

6

127

131

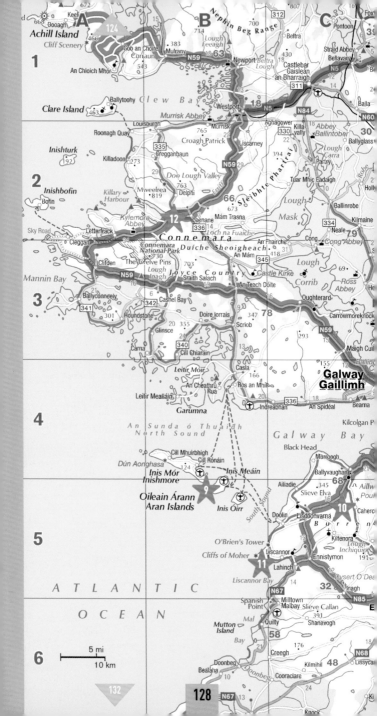

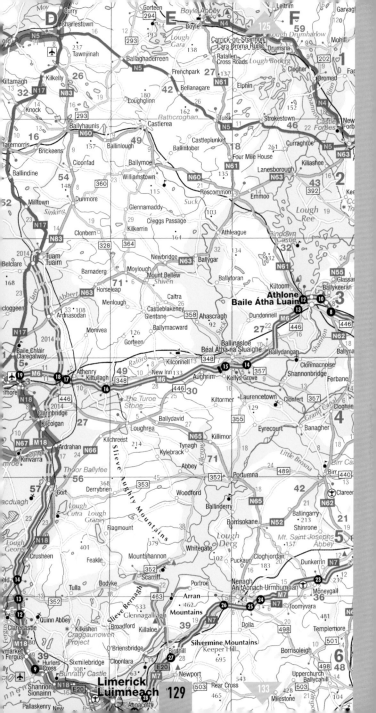

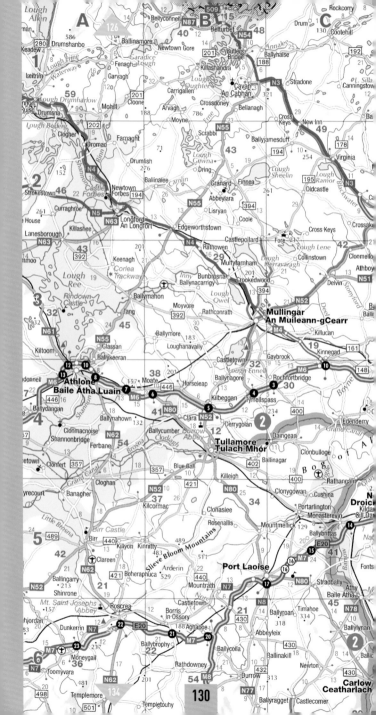

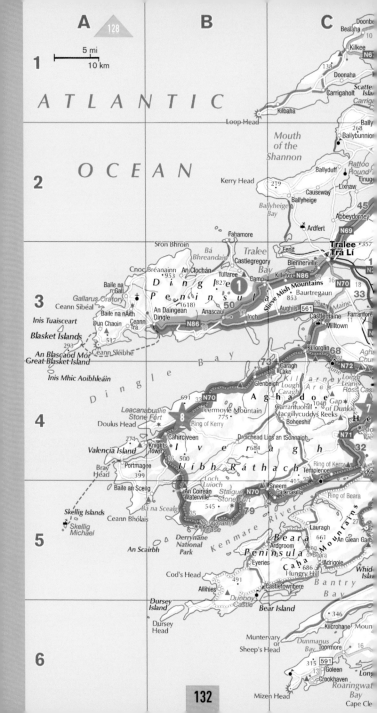

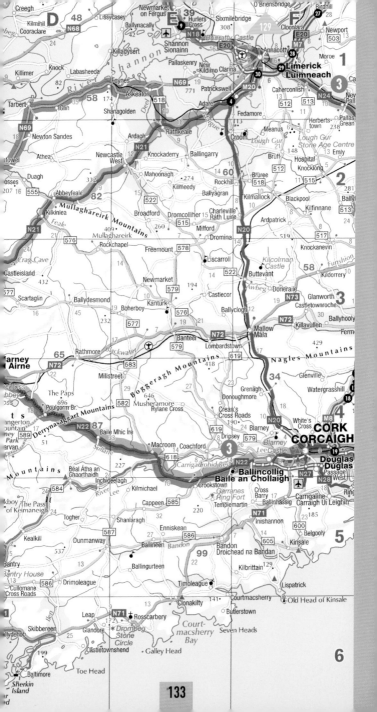

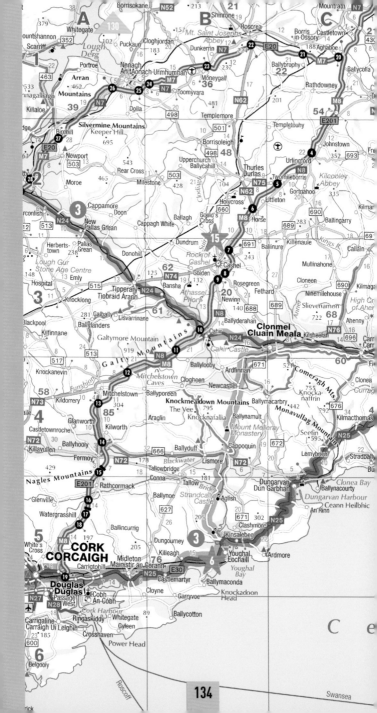

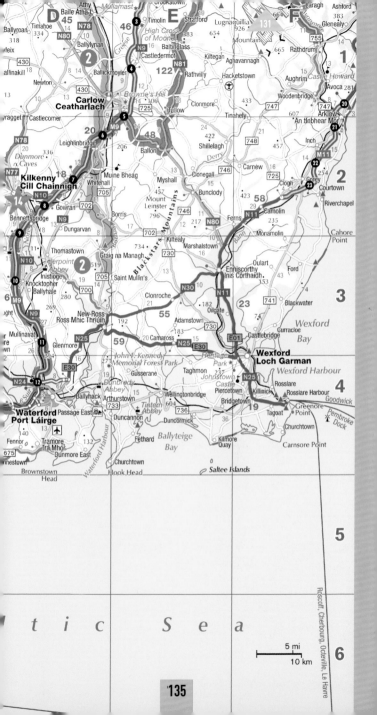

KEY TO ROAD ATLAS

18 – 26	Autobahn mit Anschlussstellen	Motorway with junctions
	Autobahn in Bau	Motorway under construction
I	Mautstelle	Toll station
	Raststätte mit Übernachtung	Roadside restaurant and hotel
	Raststätte	Roadside restaurant
	Tankstelle	Filling-station
	Autobahnähnliche Schnell-straße mit Anschlussstelle	Dual carriage-way with motorway characteristics with junction
	Fernverkehrsstraße	Trunk road
	Durchgangsstraße	Thoroughfare
	Wichtige Hauptstraße	Important main road
	Hauptstraße	Main road
	Nebenstraße	Secondary road
	Eisenbahn	Railway
	Autozug-Terminal	Car-loading terminal
	Zahnradbahn	Mountain railway
	Kabinenschwebebahn	Aerial cableway
	Eisenbahnfähre	Railway ferry
	Autofähre	Car ferry
	Schifffahrtslinie	Shipping route
	Landschaftlich besonders schöne Strecke	Route with beautiful scenery
Alleenstr.	Touristenstraße	Tourist route
XI-V	Wintersperre	Closure in winter
	Straße für Kfz gesperrt	Road closed to motor traffic
8%	Bedeutende Steigungen	Important gradients
	Für Wohnwagen nicht empfehlenswert	Not recommended for caravans
	Für Wohnwagen gesperrt	Closed for caravans
☼	Besonders schöner Ausblick	Important panoramic view

* *Wartenstein* * *Umbalfälle*	Sehenswert: Kultur - Natur	Of interest: culture - nature
	Badestrand	Bathing beach
	Nationalpark, Naturpark	National park, nature park
	Sperrgebiet	Prohibited area
	Kirche	Church
	Kloster	Monastery
	Schloss, Burg	Palace, castle
	Moschee	Mosque
	Ruinen	Ruins
	Leuchtturm	Lighthouse
	Turm	Tower
	Höhle	Cave
	Ausgrabungsstätte	Archaeological excavation
▲	Jugendherberge	Youth hostel
	Allein stehendes Hotel	Isolated hotel
	Berghütte	Refuge
▲	Campingplatz	Camping site
✈	Flughafen	Airport
✈	Regionalflughafen	Regional airport
✈	Flugplatz	Airfield
	Staatsgrenze	National boundary
	Verwaltungsgrenze	Administrative boundary
⊖	Grenzkontrollstelle	Check-point
⊖	Grenzkontrollstelle mit Beschränkung	Check-point with restrictions
ROMA	Hauptstadt	Capital
VENÉZIA	Verwaltungssitz	Seat of the administration
	Ausflüge & Touren	Trips & Tours
	Perfekte Route	Perfect route
★ 1	MARCO POLO Highlight	MARCO POLO Highlight

INDEX

This index lists all sights and destinations mentioned in the guide, as well as a few important names and terms. Page numbers in bold type refer to the main entry.

WRITE TO US

e-mail: info@marcopologuides.co.uk

Did you have a great holiday?
Is there something on your mind?
Whatever it is, let us know!
Whether you want to praise, alert us
to errors or give us a personal tip –
MARCO POLO would be pleased to
hear from you.
We do everything we can to provide
the very latest information for your trip.

Nevertheless, despite all of our authors'
thorough research, errors can creep
in. MARCO POLO does not accept any
liability for this. Please contact us by
e-mail or post.

MARCO POLO Travel Publishing Ltd
Pinewood, Chineham Business Park
Crockford Lane, Chineham
Basingstoke, Hampshire RG24 8AL
United Kingdom

PICTURE CREDITS
Cover Photograph: Patrick Pearse cottage (Getty Images/The Image Bank: Graham)
Images: W. Dieterich (40); DuMont Bildarchiv: Meinhardt (3 bottom, 10/11, 22/23, 88/89), Modrow (3 top, 36, 69, 70/71, 72, 75, 78/79, 95, 98, 100, 111, 115); Getty Images/The Image Bank: Graham (1 top); Griffin Group: Monart Destination Spa Ireland (16 top); Huber: Damm (90), Fantuz (24/25), Ripani (96/97), Spiegelhalter (44/45); Island Cottage: Tomas Tyner (17 bottom); © iStockphoto.com: Nathan Jones (16 bottom); R. Jung (4, 15); H. Krinitz (flap l., flap r., 2 centre bottom, 2 bottom, 12/13, 28, 28/29, 29, 32/33, 37, 42, 46/47, 50, 52, 54/55, 59, 63, 66, 76, 85, 106/107, 120); S. Kuttig (27, 86, 108/109, 126/127); Laif: Gonzalez (65, 110/111), Heuer (102/103), Jaenicke (2 top, 5), Krinitz (18/19, 38), Modrow (104/105), Raach (99), Zanettini (48, 56); H. Leue (7, 114 top, 114 bottom); mauritius images: Alamy (2 centre top, 6, 26 l., 30 top, 34), mauritius images/Food and Drink: Payne (26 r.); Visa Image (21); H. P. Merten (30 bottom); Slieve Aughty Centre: Victoria von Schoen (17 top); The GAA Museum (16 centre); vario images: Design Pics (82), Irish Image Collection (9, 61, 92, 110), McPHOTO (3 centre, 80/81); Visum: Achenbach & Pacini (8); White Star: Gumm (41); centre Wöbcke (1 bottom)

1st Edition 2012
Worldwide Distribution: Marco Polo Travel Publishing Ltd, Pinewood, Chineham Business Park, Crockford Lane, Basingstoke, Hampshire RG24 8AL, United Kingdom. Email: sales@marcopolouk.com
© MAIRDUMONT GmbH & Co. KG, Ostfildern
Chief editors: Michaela Lienemann (Concept, managing editor), Marion Zorn (Concept, text editor)
Author: Manfred Wöbcke, Editor: Karin Liebe
Programme supervision: Ann-Katrin Kutzner, Nikolai Michaelis, Silwen Randebrock
Picture editor: Stefan Scholtz, Gabriele Forst
What's hot: wunder media, Munich; Cartography road atlas: © MAIRDUMONT, Ostfildern
Cartography pull-out map: © MAIRDUMONT, Ostfildern
Design: milchhof : atelier, Berlin; Front cover, pull-out map cover, page 1: factor product munich
Translated from German by John Sykes; editor of the English edition: Kathleen Becker, Lisbon

DOS & DON'TS

Forgetting the raingear – or getting your long-overdue round of drinks

MISUNDERSTAND CURIOSITY

Curiosity and taking an interest in other people is second nature to the chatty Irish. Don't take it the wrong way; in this country curiosity is not a way of intruding, but signals a caring attitude towards the well-being of others – and that includes strangers.

BE TOO EASY-GOING

Ireland is a safe place, but exercise the usual precautions. There are a few areas and streets in the north of Dublin, for instance, that should be avoided at night: north of O'Connell Street, Gardiner Street and Mountjoy Square, the favourite hangouts for junkies and youth gangs. Dublin in general has seen an epidemic of iPhone robberies. Too much alcohol, at weekends in particular, can also lead to things heating up a bit in some of the more basic Dublin pubs. In this case it's best to make an ordered exit. In Northern Ireland, the official end of the Troubles has seen an increased level of race and homophobic crime.

WHAT TO WEAR IN IRELAND

The Irish might consider it a prejudice but it's kind of true: rain is always on the cards. Carry a light waterproof jacket and you won't be caught out.

GOURMET TRIPS TO KINSALE

No doubt: Kinsale is a pretty harbour town, but the hype about the self-proclaimed 'culinary capital of Ireland' is overblown. If you're coming to Kinsale for the restaurant and foodie scene, you might be disappointed. While the quality of cooking is sometimes modest, the prices seldom are.

IGNORE YELLOW LINES

Just because the Irish are easy-going doesn't mean you can park on the yellow lines on the side of the road. If you are so bold as to park on a double yellow line you might find your car gone before you're back from the chippy. And that's only the beginning of the hassle. The depot is located on the far outskirts of the city, can only be found by taxi and the fine is hefty. If you're in luck and they're open when you turn up.

FORGETTING TO PAY YOUR ROUND

The Irish are sociable and it's no secret that they love their pubs. No wonder that the usual procedure is to order a drink for the people you happen to be talking to, rather than sipping your beer on your own at the counter. The iron rule here is to stand your round after you've been treated. If you're out in a larger group make sure you don't miss your turn to buy the drinks.